Managing Project Uncertainty

For Vanessa, who shared the uncertainties along the way.

Managing Project Uncertainty

DAVID CLEDEN

Routledge
Taylor & Francis Group
LONDON AND NEW YORK

First published 2009 by Gower Publishing

Published 2016 by Routledge
2 Park Square, Milton Park, Abingdon, Oxon OX14 4RN
711 Third Avenue, New York, NY 10017, USA

Routledge is an imprint of the Taylor & Francis Group, an informa business

British Library Cataloguing in Publication Data
Cleden, David
  Managing project uncertainty. - (Advances in project management)
  1. Project management - Decision making 2. Risk management
  I. Title
  658.4'04

Library of Congress Cataloging-in-Publication Data
Cleden, David.
  Managing project uncertainty / by David Cleden.
    p. cm.
  Includes bibliographical references and index.
  ISBN 978-0-566-08840-7
  1. Project management. 2. Problem solving. 3. Uncertainty. I. Title.
  HD69.P75C5224 2009
  658.4'04--dc22

                                                                      2008046134

ISBN 13: 978-0-566-08840-7 (pbk)

CONTENTS

LIST OF FIGURES

LIST OF TABLES

STRATEGIES AND SAFETY NETS

My purpose in writing this book was twofold. Firstly, by gathering a diverse set of tools and techniques, I hoped to provide a practical way to address the kinds of uncertainty faced by project managers every day. I have seen too many well-organized, well-planned projects simply fall apart when the unexpected happens. Like you, I have thought that there must surely be better ways to avoid the pitfalls created by such uncertainty.

The second goal was to distinguish between the management of uncertainty and the narrower discipline of risk management. This may seem a subtle distinction: after all, uncertainty is the source of all risk. However, risk management largely focuses on quantifiable threats (and the actions needed to avoid or cope with their consequences), whereas managing uncertainty requires broader and more subtle approaches. It is as much to do with the threats that can't be detected, as those that can. Since some kinds of uncertainty are less susceptible to analytical techniques, managing uncertainty is a kind of alchemy: part science, part instinct, part good fortune. It is interesting to note that while many excellent texts have been written on managing risk, there are comparatively few which deal with project uncertainty.

Project managers tread a lonely path. They often bear sole responsibility for resolving all kinds of uncertainties which might otherwise be ignored in everyday life. It goes without saying that clients expect their projects to run to plan and achieve predictable outcomes, time after time. But a manager's decisions are always constrained by the juxtaposition of time, cost and quality. Often, the project manager is left to struggle for control over things which may lie beyond their influence, balancing competing demands in often rapidly changing commercial environments. If the unexpected happens, there is usually little room for manoeuvre.

Although there are no easy answers or quick fixes, uncertainty *can* be tamed. Part of the answer lies in recognizing the nature of the problem and selecting the right tool (i.e. strategy) for the job. Like any good craftsman, the project manager must be in possession of a comprehensive toolkit for managing uncertainty and – equally important – a good working knowledge of the capabilities and limitations of those tools.

INTENDED READERSHIP

The reader is assumed to be either a project management professional or a senior manager perhaps looking to extend best practice in management within an organization. Since projects come in many varieties and sizes, a project or programme manager will inevitably come to this book equipped with widely differing experiences. As such, a solid foundation in project management basics is all that is assumed, although those completely new to project management can still hope to gain important insights into the challenges ahead.

For project managers who are set in their ways, this book doesn't expect you to discard the wealth of experience and knowledge gained over the years, and it doesn't ask that you learn a new way of managing projects. Instead, it builds on what you, as an accomplished project manager, already know. It summarizes advances in project management techniques drawn from a wide range of sources. It looks at what gives rise to uncertainty and it explores the typical lifecycle of uncertainty. But most importantly, it examines a range of different strategies and looks at where they can be most effectively deployed within the uncertainty lifecycle. Through exposure to new ideas and concepts, this book will help the project manager assemble a more comprehensive management toolkit for dealing with project uncertainty.

CHAPTER 1

LIVING WITH UNCERTAINTY

Life is short, the art is long, opportunity fleeting, experiment treacherous, judgment difficult.

– Hippocrates, ancient Greek physician.

LIVING IN AN UNCERTAIN WORLD

Winston Churchill, a man not known for his lack of hubris, once wrote with the benefit of hindsight, 'I ought to have known. My advisors ought to have known and I ought to have been told, and I ought to have asked.' (Churchill 2005). In just a few words he captured both the nature of uncertainty and an important insight into how to tackle it.

Churchill was writing about a pivotal moment in the Second World War. In 1941–2 the British Government considered Singapore to be well-defended and unlikely to fall to the Japanese. It formed a vital part of the plan to bring the war in the Far East to a rapid end. Yet despite its strategic importance, little was done to explore the uncertainties underpinning these key assumptions. The reality was that Singapore was far more vulnerable to a Japanese invasion than anyone realized. Its capitulation came as a terrible blow to the Allies, although with hindsight many of the events could have been foreseen.

The modern project manager is rarely afforded the luxury of hindsight. The threats posed by uncertainty are real and immediate, and the stakes on a project are often high. The project manager faces a conundrum: decisions must be made *now* about future situations which are inherently uncertain.

It is no secret that many projects fail, regardless of the business sector. IT projects are notoriously disaster-prone, not necessarily because of technological failure but more often due to their inherent complexity. In the mid 90s, influential surveys such as those conducted by Bull and the Standish Group were reporting on average only 16 per cent of projects were classified as successful, 53 per cent were 'impaired' and 31 per cent were outright failures (for example, Bull 1998). More than a decade on, little seems to have changed. Recent surveys (for example, CA 2007) suggest that a third of all projects significantly exceed their budget. Of the reasons given, more than half of projects suffer from poor forecasting, and a third attribute problems to dependencies between multiple projects. As programmes become more ambitious and complex, the potential for uncertainty to wreak havoc only increases.

The goal of this book is to understand what gives rise to uncertainty, to recognize its symptoms and explore strategies for keeping it under control. Although uncertainty arises in many aspects of business, we will restrict the discussion to the context of uncertainty within projects, not day-to-day business uncertainty. A project differs from routine business in a number of important respects. Projects have set goals to be achieved. They have a fixed beginning and end. Within this time span, finite resources (typically measured in terms of cost and effort) must be used judiciously to achieve the objectives.

Sometimes a group of projects are initiated which will jointly achieve the broader strategic aims of a *programme* of work. Programme goals are typically ambitious – perhaps to open up a new market, or build a new infrastructure, or develop a new product. Programmes will often have co-dependent projects; therefore if a problem occurs in one place it may affect neighbouring projects and threaten the entire programme. Thus, the challenges of managing programme uncertainty are often much greater.

At the centre of this complex web of task sits the programme or project manager, marshalling and directing the available resources, and often expected to make critical decisions in less than ideal circumstances which nevertheless have far-reaching consequences.

As Churchill realized, the art of managing uncertainty depends hugely on how much we are able to understand the realities of the situation. In part, this means developing an awareness of what is known and, to some extent, what is unknown. Timeliness is also vital: it is not enough to wait to be informed. As we will see in later chapters, in order to manage project uncertainty effectively, the project manager must ask the right questions, be continually sceptical of the answers received and act where possible only on the basis of impartial evidence.

NOVELTY BREEDS UNCERTAINTY

There are no shortage of examples of projects which have got into severe difficulties in the face of overwhelming uncertainty. Many share a common feature: the pursuit of a goal never before achieved. In D.R. Myddelton's illuminating book, *They Meant Well: Government Project Disasters* he wryly observes, 'The frontiers of knowledge ... are also the frontiers of ignorance.' (Myddelton 2007)

Ambitious projects are commonplace in modern business. Increased competition drives businesses to set up more daring projects to win market share or explore new operational domains. To cope with these changes, organizational structures have to become more fluid. Plus, the speed of change in business means an inevitable shift away from the safe, repeatable ways of working towards highly original and innovative projects – what some researchers (for example, Loch, DeMeyer and Pich 2006) refer to as *novel* projects.

A novel project breaks the mould. It often ventures into unfamiliar areas of technology, process or marketplace. A novel project confronts situations for which there is little prior knowledge or experience to act as a guide. This is where the dangers posed by uncertainty are at their greatest.

Mission to Jupiter

John Casani knows a thing or two about novel projects. For more than a decade in the late 70s and early 80s, he was the project manager for NASA's flagship space exploration project, the Galileo mission. Coordinating multi-disciplinary teams of scientists and engineers from every continent, he steered the project through political infighting, budgetary crises and overcame numerous technical and engineering uncertainties (Meltzer 2007).

The challenges were immense. Galileo's main objective was to travel more than 2.4 billion miles and enter a precise orbit around Jupiter, dropping a scientific instrument package through Jupiter's atmosphere and relaying vast quantities of data back to mission control. The navigational task alone was likened to 'firing an arrow from Los Angeles to New York and missing the bull's-eye by six inches.' In such a remote, hostile environment, plenty of uncertainty remained even after decades of planning and preparation. Just one tiny problem during the journey could wreck the entire programme.

There was also plenty of uncertainty to contend with back on Earth. On no less than four separate occasions, the project was threatened with cancellation. After years of planning, the unexpected loss of the Challenger shuttle forced the team to use a less powerful upper stage rocket. It meant Galileo could not reach Jupiter unless it performed a complicated (and risky) series of gravity-assist flybys.

Then as Galileo finally approached Jupiter, the programme hit its most serious problem: a high gain antenna providing the vital data link back to Earth failed to deploy properly. Without the science data, the mission would be a failure. Eventually, the team were able to reconfigure a secondary antenna and drip-feed most of the data back, though only at painfully slow speeds.

What makes the Galileo programme such an interesting case study is not just the enormous efforts that went in to finding and eliminating uncertainty, but the resilience of the programme when problems did occur. Right from the start the Galileo team built the programme around strategies which allowed it to respond to the unexpected, even capitalizing in some cases on opportunities that presented themselves. One of Casani's successors, Eilene Theilig said, 'I really like watching people presented with a problem, and using their creativity to overcome it. And we've had lots of examples of that.'

In the light of these lessons, later chapters will examine more closely how a project can develop greater resilience to uncertainty.

RISK VERSUS UNCERTAINTY

In common use, words such as *doubt, uncertainty, risk* and *ambiguity* are often used interchangeably, but to develop a detailed understanding of why uncertainty arises and how it can be controlled, we need clearer definitions. (Refer to the *Glossary* for more detail.) Crucially, there is an important distinction between risk and uncertainty. It is easy to fall into the trap of thinking that by managing risk we are also managing uncertainty: the two are not the same.

Let us first examine what we mean by *risk*. A risk has the following attributes:

- For a risk to exist, we must be able to *conceive* of the threat it embodies.
- A risk can be *quantified*, usually in terms of the likelihood and severity of its consequences, but sometimes in more tangible ways.
- A risk describes a *vulnerability*. By analysing a risk we build up a better picture of where the project is vulnerable and its implications.
- If a risk can be identified, so can a *mitigation plan* (that is, a sequence of events which will either reduce the likelihood of the risk occurring, or reduce its consequences if it does occur). However, we may choose not to follow a mitigation plan if it is not deemed to be cost-effective.

Notice that for a risk to be identified, we must have a basic level of knowledge concerning the problem. What is the threat? What impact might it have? Where is the project vulnerable and how might we fix this? This is a knowledge-centric view. If there are sufficiently important things we don't know, these can be represented as a series of risks for the project.

Uncertainty is much less susceptible to analysis; it is what is left behind when all the risks have been identified. Uncertainty represents a threat, but we cannot be sure what form it takes otherwise we would identify it as a risk. We may be able to see that there is a gap in our understanding but unlike a risk, we don't know what it is we don't know. Not until uncertainty manifests itself into a specific problem is the nature of the threat revealed – and by then it may be too late to deal effectively with the consequences.

Many writers (for example, Chapman and Ward 2003 and Loch, DeMeyer and Pich 2006) define uncertainty as the *source* of risk. Extending this idea a little further, we can derive the following relationship:

- uncertainty is the intangible measure of what we don't know;
- risk is the statement of what may arise from that lack of knowledge.

It follows that two kinds of uncertainty exist: the kind that we start out with before we make any attempt at analysing the risks, (which we will call *inherent uncertainty*) and the uncertainty that remains once all the risks have been identified (which we will call *latent uncertainty*). This means that the process of risk analysis (that is, the steps taken to identify and quantify project risks) transforms some – but not all – of the inherent uncertainty into risks. What remains is latent uncertainty (see Figure 1.1).

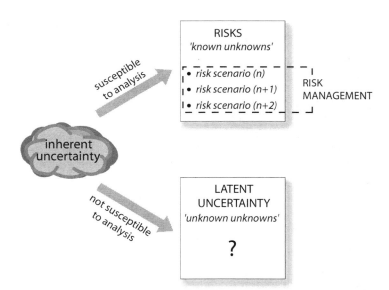

Figure 1.1   The relationship between risk and uncertainty. *Risks can be identified by analysing the inherent uncertainty of a project. But inevitably some uncertainty remains, no matter how thorough the analysis. This is termed* 'latent uncertainty'.

Risk management is a vital tool. It reduces the overall level of uncertainty associated with the project. There are many well-established risk management techniques which, if correctly applied, can successfully manage the threat embodied in these risks. However, risk management by itself is not enough and is limited in several ways:

- in complex projects, risk management quickly becomes resource-intensive;
- errors of judgment in prioritizing risks can introduce vulnerability;
- it can't handle unforeseen situations (that is, those commonly encountered in novel projects).

Risk management works best where uncertainty is quantifiable, that is, where risks can be conceived of, analysed, understood and planned for. But not all kinds of uncertainty are that obliging.

The limits of risk management

A project manager who relies solely on risk management may labour under the false impression that all the unknowns are being addressed. As Figure 1.1 shows, some uncertainty is not susceptible to risk analysis. Thus latent uncertainty can manifest as a problem much later in the project, often without warning. Since it does not appear on the project's risk register, the project may be ill-equipped to deal with it.

There is a further limit to the risk management process. Unless the project has virtually unlimited resources, risk management processes are typically only applied to a subset of the potential risks. The project manager is forced to take a pragmatic approach, categorizing risks, prioritizing those which represent the greatest threat, and deploying resources accordingly. If this judgment is faulty or the risks change over time, risk management may be ineffectual.

Therefore, risk management can only address the following subset of risks:

- those that we can conceive of;
- those that we have the resources to analyse;
- those that we have the resources to mitigate and track.

So at best, risks can only be drawn up against a quite limited subset of actual threats to the project. Whereas risks always arise from uncertainty, not all uncertainty can be expressed as a set of risks. Crucially, risk analysis alone cannot encompass the entire range of threats to a project even though many of the techniques for managing risk and managing uncertainty are synonymous.

Uncertainty and risk management must therefore be considered complementary approaches. Strategies which reduce inherent uncertainty 'at source' will reduce the workload in capturing, analysing and mitigating risks. Whilst risk management remains an important tool, the project manager also needs strategies for managing uncertainty, that is, dealing with the areas which risk management cannot touch.

For the record, we will not look at risk management processes in any depth. There are many excellent books which explore this topic; for further guidance see the recommendations under *Recommended Reading*. Instead, we will focus our attention on managing uncertainty – a much more neglected and frequently misunderstood topic.

VARIABILITY AND INDETERMINACY

The first step towards managing uncertainty is to recognize what we are dealing with. Uncertainty can be grouped into two main classes:

1. variability;
2. indeterminacy.

Variable uncertainty is forward looking. Because there is variability, it gives rise to a set of possible outcomes. An obvious example is turning over a playing card. The outcome must be one of 52 possibilities. Although we may be able to identify the possible scenarios, the difficulty is knowing which is the right one. Unless we make the right choice, our project plan may still turn out to be based on faulty assumptions.

Variable uncertainty is behind many common problems – for example, accurately predicting when a project milestone will be achieved. Many different variables are at work: for example, the work rate of the production team, whether or not suppliers meet their deadlines and the quality of the outputs, etc. If all goes well, the milestone could be reached by month nine – but if the worst happens, it could slip to month 15. All we can say with certainty is that the milestone will fall somewhere between these extremes, but variability makes it difficult to be certain of the actual date.

Indeterminate uncertainty always leads to ambiguity. It may be impossible to identify the set of future scenarios, perhaps because we don't understand the underlying processes sufficiently. It can also mean an inability to explain the sequence of events leading up to the present situation. With indeterminate uncertainty, we can't narrow down the outcomes to a set of choices: it is like trying to predict what is written on a business card before turning it over.

UNCERTAIN OUTCOMES

Uncertainty is not always a bad thing. As Figure 1.2 shows, it gives rise to three kinds of outcome:

1. threats and unexpected events;
2. irrelevant consequences;
3. opportunities.

The threat from uncertainty is often at the forefront of a project manager's mind, but a lot of uncertainty gives rise to events and situations which have no bearing on the project's objectives. Worrying about this kind of uncertainty is unproductive. Why waste resources on something that represents no threat? However, isolating irrelevant uncertainty can be difficult and depends on developing a deep understanding of the relationship between many different project factors.

Furthermore, some uncertainty actually creates new opportunities. Sometimes the act of resolving uncertainty may suggest new possibilities or lead to the discovery of alternatives not previously considered. Many important discoveries have been made while probing into areas of uncertainty. The history of technological and scientific progress is littered with examples of such unexpected discoveries: for example, Alexander Fleming's realization that, far from his experiment failing, the contaminated petri dish he was about to discard contained an extremely useful anti-bacterial substance (penicillin).

This brings us to the first of our guiding principles for managing uncertainty: *Uncertainty encompasses both opportunity and threat.* The plans that we formulate need to take account of both.

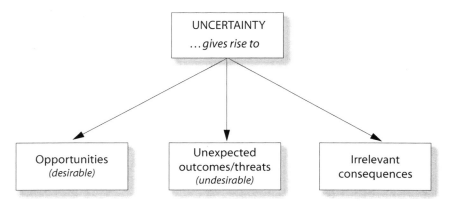

Figure 1.2   Uncertain outcomes. *Far from being all bad, much of the uncertainty may be irrelevant to the project or may even have benefits.*

THE KNOWLEDGE-CENTRIC VIEW OF UNCERTAINTY

Uncertainty is often used as a collective term for a wide variety of issues: missing data, faulty assumptions, imprecise measurements, variability in key drivers, lack of knowledge, poor communication, and misunderstood principles. Consider the sort of questions that bombard a project manager on a typical day (see Table 1.1). Although the uncertainty takes many different forms, each of these examples has something in common: a lack of knowledge of some vital aspect of the project.

Table 1.1   Observed uncertainty

Question	What's missing
Will this supplier deliver the critical component when I need it?	Knowledge of an external dependency, that is, unknown reliability of the supplier.
How long will this task take?	No planning metrics or ambiguous estimation methods.
How will the client react to the proposed designs?	Hard to predict client behaviour/ uncertain nature of the relationship.
How can I be sure the production equipment is reliable?	Unknown assessment criteria.
Why is there an upward trend in the defect rate?	Flawed models or lack of understanding of key drivers.
How could this failure have occurred?	Limited knowledge of cause-and-effect chains.
What does these statistics mean?	Ambiguous data or lack of an effective forecasting model.
Are we keeping to plan	Lack of progress information.
What might happen to the project in a month's time?	Insufficient data to forecast future events

We can go further and identify different categories of missing knowledge which characterize uncertainty:

- uncertain information;
- uncertain understanding;
- uncertain tempo;
- uncertain complexity.

Uncertain information

The lack of good information or data is often what springs to mind when we think about uncertainty. Accurate information is needed for all sorts of activities – good decision-making, planning assumptions, basis for estimation, specification of requirements, management of stakeholder relationships, etc. It follows that when information is inherently uncertain or is simply unavailable, it can have far-reaching effects.

Gathering all the relevant facts is synonymous with certainty. Without them, we are left in the dark, facing considerable uncertainty.

Uncertain understanding

John Naisbitt wrote, 'We are drowning in information but starved for knowledge.' Although gathering information is a good starting point, understanding how it all fits together is equally important. It may be as simple as the order in which project tasks need to be done, the effect of an action on other interlinked tasks, or which activities have the greatest influence on the outcome of the project. These task relationships and dependencies play a key part in determining whether progress is made, and how quickly.

Most project managers either consciously or unconsciously build a model of how project events will develop over time. At its simplest, the model tells us that requirements need to be finalized before design begins, that development precedes testing, that incorporating feedback from a pilot deployment may lead to higher user satisfaction in the long term, etc. More complex models capture much more detail about the relationships between different parts of the project, the influencing factors (that is, drivers) and all the external dependencies. Many models also consider how external factors affect the project. This often provides the context which determines how success will be measured.

If the model is a good one, the project manager can use it to wind the clock forward and make accurate predictions about future scenarios. For example: what resources need to be deployed to support delivery? What demands will be placed on the client's organization? Where will the bottlenecks occur? What happens to these deadlines if a certain task runs late?

The better the understanding of the underlying relationships, the easier it is for the project manager to spot trouble and avoid it in time. An uncertain understanding leads to a flawed model, so we can't be sure our predictions are correct. Without this certainty, we may be planning for the wrong eventuality, or get caught out by an unexpected outcome.

Uncertain tempo

Even when our understanding of the project permits us to forecast scenarios with reasonable certainty, the pace of events can catch us out. An uncertain tempo means we can predict the *what* but not the *when*. If things happen much faster than expected, we are forced to make hasty or ill-informed decisions. Without enough time to prepare properly, instead of managing the problem away, it starts to gain momentum and may escalate into a crisis.

Sometimes the tempo of uncertainty means that a situation develops much more slowly than expected. This can be equally damaging: things don't go according to plan, more resources are consumed than were estimated, and incomplete tasks start to stack up.

It is important to understand the tempo of uncertainty because only then can we address questions such as:

- How much time is there to resolve the uncertainty? (Or: how long before the uncertainty transitions into an undesirable event?)
- When is the right time to act?

It is tempting to address key areas of uncertainty immediately they are detected. However, in the resource-constrained circumstances of a typical project, this may not be sensible. As we will see in Chapter 2, there is a trade-off between choosing to act or not, and determining when is the most effective time to act is vital. Delayed action may seem counter-intuitive but it is always worth considering if, by gathering more information, it is possible to arrive at a better long term solution.

When a major IT firm with a large contract to supply secure communications infrastructure to Government learnt that a key supplier was unlikely to meet demand for sufficient volumes of a core component, the initial reaction was to concentrate on finding a replacement supplier. In such a niche market, this was not straightforward. After careful consideration, the management team devised an alternative strategy. Since the production phase of the project was still months in the future, the design team were instructed to explore alternative designs which circumvented this particular component. In due course, a better design was developed – one that not only avoided dependency on the unreliable supplier, but actually provided better inherent security. By realizing there was time to consider alternatives, the project ended up benefiting from this particular uncertainty.

Uncertain complexity

Many uncertain situations can only be dealt with effectively once the complexities are fully understood. This means being able to predict what consequences will arise from a certain course of action and what relationships exist between key drivers. It also means being able to explain why certain events have occurred.

If there are hidden complexities – or if there is no clear explanation of why a given event has occurred – it may be very hard to find the right solution to the problem. A doctor who only treats the patient's symptoms may be unable to effect a long term cure and the patient's condition may worsen. However, understanding the root of the illness – and therefore being able to explain why the symptoms have – arisen is likely to deliver a cure that is targeted at the real problem, not just its symptoms.

Failure to address complexity often leads to a crisis being mismanaged. By not understanding why an unexpected situation has arisen, there is a risk of making things worse. For the project manager, analysing the complexities and underlying causes of an uncertain situation is a vital prerequisite to handling a crisis. If our understanding of these complex relationships is uncertain, so is the outcome.

THE 'FOUR QUADRANTS' MODEL

This knowledge-centric view of uncertainty doesn't just generate a binary outcome where something is either *known* (that is, a certainty) or *not known* (that is, an uncertainty). In fact, there are four possibilities, leading to the *Four Quadrants* model.

Often we may be aware that key knowledge is missing. For example, the plan may call for a key subcomponent to be provided on a certain date but the project manager hasn't established if the manufacturer can meet the deadline. Thus the likely delivery date is unknown – but we know this information is missing. These kind of uncertainties are often termed 'known unknowns.'

We can go further. Any uncertainty of the 'known unknown' kind can be further investigated and, if we choose (and providing it makes economic sense) can be framed as a risk. Even though known unknowns can be a major source of worry for a project manager, the tools to deal with them are readily available in the form of risk management processes.

Communication problems and poor knowledge sharing practices gives rise to a different kind of knowledge problem. It is common for knowledge, skills and experience needed by the project to exist within an organization without the project team realizing. We talk about a project 'reinventing the wheel' when all that is needed is to tap into readily available resources elsewhere. Following the logic of the previous categories, these are the 'unknown knowns' representing untapped information resources. This kind of uncertainty typically doesn't threaten the successful outcome of a project in the same way that 'known unknowns' do, but it points to missed opportunities to benefit from knowledge that is there for the taking. Failing to take advantage of corporate knowledge can be costly. It is the reason why the field of knowledge management has grown to be enormously important in recent years.

The fourth quadrant is the hardest to deal with and concerns the 'unknown unknowns' or what we might call *unfathomable* uncertainty. Inside this category sit all the things that the project manager does not know about in advance, including what some researchers refer to as 'bolts from the blue' (Kylen 1985) which are, by definition, impossible to predict. Very often, all we can say is that a project has a high capacity for this kind of uncertainty (as is the case in a novel project) but the nature of these uncertainties remains elusive.

Figure 1.3 shows a simplified view of the knowledge-centric model of uncertainty. Regardless of the business context, a project will be comprised of four quadrants:

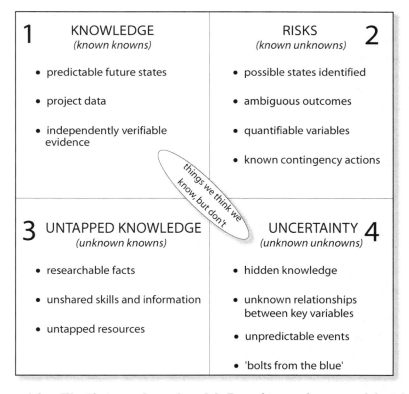

Figure 1.3   The 'four quadrants' model. *Everything we know – and don't know – about the project fits into one of these quadrants.*

- knowledge (that is, facts) – things which are known (and ideally, independently verified);
- untapped knowledge – information that can be researched or wisdom that can be unlocked if only we knew how;
- risks – gaps in knowledge which we think constitute a threat to the project;
- latent uncertainty – gaps in our knowledge we may not even be aware of.

Sometimes we are misled by facts – things that we think we know, but don't. These items start out in quadrant 1 (known knowns) but later turn out to be not as we perceived them. Obvious examples are incorrect assumptions, erroneous planning data, inaccurate metrics, misunderstood requirements and misjudged competencies. There is a potent danger attached to this subset because just like the uncertainty of quadrant 4, we don't know that such uncertainty exists until it reveals itself. So even our 'known knowns' in quadrant 1 are not totally immune from uncertainty.

Quadrant 4 – at the heart of uncertainty

The heart of managing uncertainty is determined by how we deal with issues in quadrant 4. Since we can only act on the basis of what we know, what we think we know, or where we recognize there are gaps in our knowledge, this is quite a challenge. Gaps in our knowledge and understanding can be filled, given time and resources, but only if we know that such uncertainty exists. But what can we do about uncertainties that we are not even aware of?

The uncertainty of quadrant 4 is *unfathomable* because it has one or both of these properties:

- Type 1 unfathomability – We have no knowledge of its *existence* (although if we did, we might be able to do something about it).
- Type 2 unfathomability – We have no way to measure, categorize or comprehend the uncertainty, even if we are aware of its existence.

In the latter case, do not confuse knowing that a situation is unfathomable with knowledge of the nature of the uncertainty. Someone may tell us that a terrible danger lurks behind a locked door, but we still have no idea (and no practical way of finding out) what uncertainty faces us if we unlock the door and enter. We know the situation is unfathomable but we don't know what it is that we don't know. In other words, the future is still unforeseeable.

How then can we tackle unfathomable uncertainty? In the case of type 1 unfathomability, discovering its existence is key. It means going looking for uncertainty even in places where we don't expect to find it. We may not be able to solve the underlying problem, but at least we are now in a position to understand the uncertainty a little better. By discovering something of the existence and nature of the uncertainty, it moves us out of quadrant 4 and into quadrant 2 where we can use analytical techniques such as risk management to lay bare the problem and deal with it appropriately.

Something different is needed for dealing with the second type of unfathomability. There are two main strategies:

1. multiple explorations;
2. fast learning loops.

By conducting a series of experiments over time, we can gather more information, for example, by revealing key drivers and their interrelationships. Naturally, some of the experiments will fail, but both failure and success says something about the nature of the underlying uncertainty. By studying the outcome of the experiments we can start to understand the sources of uncertainty and build a new (or better) predictive model.

Technologists do this all the time: they build a prototype, observe its behaviour under test, and learn where there are key uncertainties. Armed with this knowledge, another prototype is built, repeating the process and gradually eliminating the unexpected outcomes.

This kind of exploration is often used to tackle one of the commonest examples of project uncertainty: estimating project duration. Since there are no metrics or previous experience to fall back on in a highly novel project, accurate estimation is difficult. One way is to identify a representative subtask and build (or prototype) the desired outputs. By observing how long the subtask takes (and what kinds of problems are encountered), the project manager gathers sufficient information to scale this performance up across the entire activity, arriving at a better estimate for the full project duration.

The second strategy, *fast learning loops*, is less straight-forward and can be risky. It requires the project to take a series of small, tentative steps and react quickly to the problems which are inevitably encountered. The negative effects of uncertainty are not avoided, but are dealt with in small doses. The success of fast learning loops depends largely on agility, flexibility, mindset, and being fully attuned to the project's objectives. We will explore this further in Chapter 6.

ADOPTING A STRUCTURED APPROACH TO MANAGING UNCERTAINTY

The uncertainty lifecycle

Over the course of a project, uncertainty follows a typical lifecycle, as shown in Figure 1.4. By understanding this lifecycle, we can adopt appropriate strategies to deal with it at each stage.

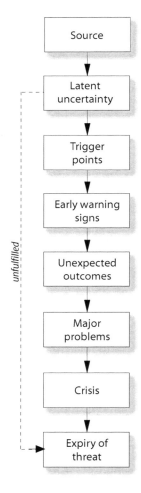

Figure 1.4   The uncertainty lifecycle. *Latent uncertainty, once triggered, has the potential to develop into unexpected outcomes, giving rise to major problems or creating a crisis. However, some latent uncertainty may remain unfulfilled during the lifetime of the project.*

It begins with a *source* of uncertainty. We may not always be aware of the source (as with the 'bolt from the blue' situation) but hindsight will usually reveal its existence. If detected early enough, *anticipation strategies* can be used to contain the uncertainty at source. Anticipating uncertainty often means trying to learn more about the nature of the uncertainty, for example, by framing the problem it represents or modelling future scenarios and preparing for them. Using *discovery techniques* such as constructing a knowledge map of what is and isn't known about a particular issue will often highlight aspects of unfathomable uncertainty. Once a source of uncertainty is revealed, analytical techniques such as risk management can be used to draw the uncertainty across into quadrant 2.

The direct threat to a project's objectives often occurs relatively late in the lifecycle. While latent uncertainty represents a threat, the real difficulty for the project manager occurs when this triggers some unexpected event. For example, not until two components are integrated does it become apparent that incorrect manufacturing tolerances have been used. Latent uncertainty (that is, the manufacturing tolerance) triggers an unexpected outcome (that is, a bad fit) only at the point of integration.

This trigger may be accompanied by early warning signs: if the project is particularly 'aware' it may be possible to respond swiftly and contain the problem even without prior knowledge of the uncertainty, either by recognizing the inherent risk or by removing the source of uncertainty before it has a chance to develop.

It is also worth remembering that many kinds of uncertainty will never undergo the transition to create an unexpected outcome. Once again, the economic argument (that it is neither desirable nor possible to eliminate all uncertainty from a project) is a powerful one. The goal is to focus sufficient effort on the areas of uncertainty that represent the greatest threat and have the highest chance of developing into serious problems.

Strategies for managing uncertainty

In the following chapters, we will examine a number of strategies for managing uncertainty. Some of these aim to restrict the source of uncertainty, thereby reducing the likelihood of problems arising. Some deal with the consequences of uncertainty which have already manifested into unexpected events. Most projects require a blend of these strategies to manage uncertainty effectively.

As the uncertainty lifecycle shows, we can use different strategies at different stages in the lifecycle (see Figure 1.5):

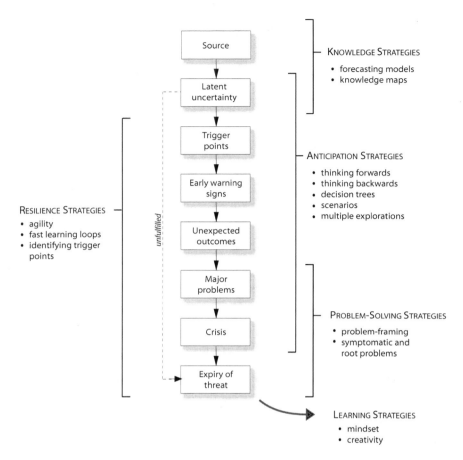

Figure 1.5   The uncertainty lifecycle overlaid with the key types of strategy

- **knowledge-centric strategies**: help to discover the sources of uncertainty, resolve them where possible, or prepare appropriately, for example, through mitigation planning and risk management.
- **anticipation strategies**: offer a more holistic approach than the knowledge-centred view of uncertainty. By looking at a project from different perspectives, visualizing future scenarios and examining causal relationships, previously hidden uncertainties are revealed.
- **resilience strategies**: trying to contain uncertainty at source will never be 100 per cent successful. Therefore, a project needs resilience and must be able to detect and respond rapidly to unexpected events. Whilst it is impossible to predict the nature of the problem in advance, project

managers can employ strategies which will imbue their projects with much greater resilience.

- **learning strategies**: give the project manager, and the organization as a whole, the ability to improve and benefit from experience over time. No two projects face exactly the same uncertainty, therefore it is important to be able to adapt lessons learned over time.

CHAPTER 2

UNCERTAINTY IN PROJECT AND PROGRAMME PLANS

The information you have is not the information you want. The information you want is not the information you need. The information you need is not the information you can obtain. The information you can obtain costs more than you want to pay.

– Finagle's Laws of Information,
from *Against the Gods: The Remarkable Story of Risk*, by Peter Bernstein.

We have established that uncertainty can arise from deficiencies in several different areas of knowledge such as contextual information about the project, our understanding of underlying processes, explanations of past events and the speed of change (or tempo). But where do these factors come into play within the typical project? What aspects of a project plan are particularly vulnerable to each type of uncertainty?

To answer these questions, we first have to look at what elements make up a typical project. Then we examine what happens as the scale and complexity of the model increases.

TRADEOFFS AND AFFORDABILITY

Can you afford to be certain?

The problem with removing uncertainties (even just those that we can conceive of) is that it is expensive. It takes time (and therefore money) to gather missing information, explore different paths, model future scenarios and to put contingency plans in place. If the stakes are high and the project objectives demand it, a strongly risk-averse strategy may be called for, but it always comes at a high price. Depending on what level of risk is considered acceptable, there is a threshold where it becomes uneconomic to tackle further uncertainty.

On the other hand, whilst doing nothing is certainly a cheap option, it leaves the project exposed to expensive problems later on. Somewhere in between these extremes lies a zone of affordable protection (see Figure 2.1).

It is tempting to want to eliminate all uncertainty, but the enormous levels of resources needed to even come close to this goal are, in all but the most exceptional cases, unwarranted. Indeed, huge efforts on eradicating sources of uncertainty often divert attention away from the real goals. Eradication is rarely the answer, whereas it remains much more feasible to contain uncertainty within acceptable levels. This leads to another guiding principle for managing uncertainty: *The goal is containment of uncertainty, not elimination.*

In pursuit of perfection

The naïve project manager believes that by strictly 'obeying the rules' of project management, uncertainty is eliminated at the outset. In other words, by 'doing the right things' (as defined by the chosen management methodology) and doing them with sufficient rigour and thoroughness, unexpected problems will be avoided.

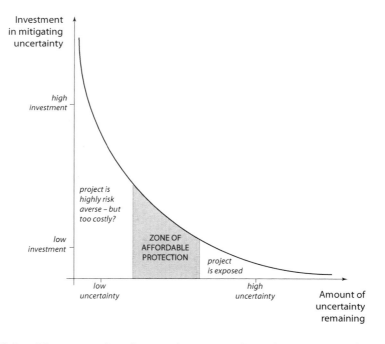

Figure 2.1   The economics of managing uncertainty. *Attempts to eradicate all programme uncertainty will be expensive. Knowing the limits of the zone of affordable protection will dictate which strategies to use.*

Thus uncertainty only remains where we have failed to apply the methodology thoroughly.

This kind of brute force mentality suggests that we must conceive of and evaluate each possible scenario, in order to identify the complete set of risks. Then risk management processes must be put in place to prevent these risks occurring and hence eliminate the threat of uncertainty.

But we have already seen that the economics of most projects force a tradeoff to be made between the cost of containing uncertainty and the damage likely to be caused to the project. Prioritizing major risks is a positive step, but how can we be sure that the right risks have been prioritized? And what about the unknown uncertainties, the bolts from the blue?

Some kinds of uncertainty simply cannot be addressed via an analytical approach. It may be that the chance superposition of a series of random events combine to deliver an unexpected result. Pharmaceutical companies have longed wrestled with this problem. Despite extensive testing programmes, there is always the risk of some unlikely combination of environmental factors (typically other medicines being taken by the patient) reacting to cause harmful side-effects.

Classical management methods cannot prevent these kinds of unexpected problems. No matter how much effort is put in, no matter how many stones we turn over, the potential for uncertainty remains. It leads to a third guiding principle for managing uncertainty: *The existence of uncertainty is not due to an inherent failure to execute project management processes thoroughly.*

It is important to realize that some uncertainty will remain no matter how thoroughly the project is planned. Conversely, it is not a sign of weak management to acknowledge that uncertainty exists within a project.

PROJECT COMPLEXITY

An assessment of the inherent complexity of a project is usually a good indicator of how much latent uncertainty there is in the project. The measure of project complexity depends on two things:

1. the number of project elements;
2. the number and nature of interactions between elements.

A large project has many different elements: many different tasks to be performed, deliverables to be produced, subcontractor inputs to be controlled, a large team to be managed, etc. But this is only one dimension of complexity: if these elements interact with each other and have non-trivial dependencies, it creates a complex set of interrelationships. Changes to one part of the system may have large or hard to predict consequences for other parts of the project.

The simplest type of interaction is sequential: task B cannot begin until task A is completed, and so on down the line. Therefore unexpected delays in completing task A will have schedule implications for following tasks unless we have allowed some 'slack' in the plan. As the number of dependent tasks increases, a complex network of dependencies quickly develops. Software engineers use the term tightly coupled for system components which have direct and immediate consequences on each other. These exhibit elaborate interconnections, where changing one variable may have unpredictable consequences in other parts of the system. Unlike a production line which is essentially a set of sequential interactions, dynamic and non-linear feedback mechanisms often exist. Hence the fourth guiding principle for managing uncertainty: *Uncertainty is an attribute, not an entity in its own right.*

Uncertainty has no independent existence; it is not an object which can be identified, trapped and eliminated like a virus invading the living organism of our project. Uncertainty naturally arises out of complex situations and is therefore an integral part of most projects. It is simply an expression of a project's ambiguity and indeterminism in the same way that the colour yellow is an attribute of a daffodil but is not a discrete or separable part of the flower.

This means that our defense mechanisms against uncertainty must be based on a better understanding of how the project's constituent parts function. Gaining that understanding provides two things: clues as to where there are gaps in our knowledge, and a clearer idea of what 'normal' looks like on the project. The first element points to potential sources of uncertainty, and the second gives us a reference point to detect deviations from the norm – early warning signs of the unexpected.

Compartmentalizing uncertainty

One of the by-products of breaking a project up into a sequence of tasks (that is, developing a workflow) is that key uncertainties are compartmentalized. By this we mean that there are natural breakpoints or gateways which can only be passed when certain targets have been reached. Clearly, no project manager wants to hit major (and possibly insurmountable) problems right at the end of the project; the aim is always to reduce the risks from uncertainty over time. By compartmentalizing uncertainty, the project deals with different types of uncertainty at different stages, the aim being not to carry forward too much uncertainty from one stage to the next and, in particular, to avoid nasty surprises near the end of the project where there is often little time or budget left to respond.

A project lifecycle splits into stages according to one of two principles:

1. sequential delivery (where similar tasks are grouped together in a stage according to a logical sequence of work);
2. incremental delivery (where project outputs are iteratively refined in successive stages, that is, mini versions of the logical sequence are repeated).

The sequentialist argues that by grouping together similar types of activities, the uncertainties associated with these tasks can be collected together and dealt with at the appropriate point in the schedule (see Figure 2.2). Suppose a client is uncertain of their detailed requirements. The project manager forces major uncertainties to be confronted early on by asking the client to agree a detailed specification. Until this is done, other aspects of the project are put on hold. Although the project may be delayed while these uncertainties are addressed, subsequent tasks can be undertaken knowing that any uncertainties in the specification have been contained within acceptable levels.

Furthermore, gateway checks and reviews between stages help to ensure that core uncertainties are resolved before the project can progress. This avoids uncertainty rolling forwards into future stages, like a snowball gathering momentum down the side of a mountain.

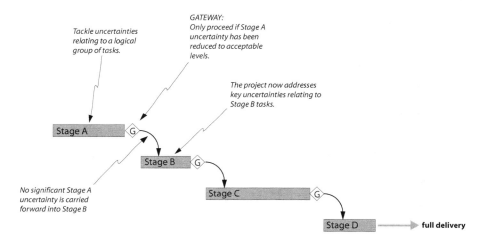

Figure 2.2   Managing uncertainty in a sequential delivery cycle. *Gateway reviews between each stage prevent critical areas of uncertainty from being carried forward into the next stage.*

The incrementalist takes a different view. Many projects are delivered into a dynamic environment where many factors – including the project's objectives – are liable to change. Therefore it is unreasonable to expect detailed specifications to remain unaltered between project inception and delivery – a period which might span months, if not years. Even if requirements don't change, the client and the project team may lack a sufficiently clear understanding of the objectives and business benefits at the start of the project. This needs time to evolve, and for both parties to develop a common expectation of what the project will deliver.

As Figure 2.3 shows, incremental delivery provides some flexibility to address these uncertainties by gradually refining an initial set of outputs created early on in the project. Lessons learnt from these early deliveries are fed back into the next cycle, enabling plans and strategies (and even the project's objectives, in some cases) to be fine-tuned. This approach identifies major uncertainties associated with the latter stage of work much earlier, so that the project has time to respond and adapt, either reducing or avoiding key areas of uncertainty altogether.

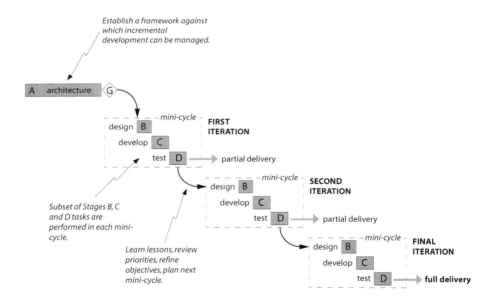

Figure 2.3   Managing uncertainty in an incremental delivery process. *Key areas of uncertainty are reduced through successive iterations of 'mini-cycles' of the project. These enable the project to adapt as uncertainty is encountered in each cycle.*

CAPACITY FOR UNCERTAINTY

Each project will have a different capacity for uncertainty. This is a measure of how much uncertainty the project can tolerate. High risk projects, that is, typically novel projects which are pursuing ambitious goals where it is accepted that the likelihood of failure is high, will have a high capacity for uncertainty. Major uncertainties will be tolerated because the potential rewards justify it and – equally important – the consequences of failure can be endured. High risk projects with a high capacity for uncertainty are a gamble, but one that the project stakeholders must understand and be prepared to sign up to.

If lives are at stake or the consequences of failure are unpalatable, a project will have a low capacity for uncertainty. Each area of uncertainty represents a threat and must therefore be reduced by whatever methods are available.

Table 2.1 describes both ends of the scale. Most projects have a capacity for uncertainty which falls somewhere inbetween. For example, the construction of a new road bridge is likely to have a low capacity for uncertainty. No one wants to drive across a bridge if the engineers are uncertain about its load-bearing performance, or don't know if the concrete was poured properly, or whether wind shear was modelled correctly. Conversely, a research and development project which might conceivably result in a revolutionary new product has a high capacity for uncertainty (and is highly novel). There is a strong possibility of failure, but the potential benefits of success make the attempt worthwhile.

A project with a low capacity for uncertainty may require a more costly uncertainty strategy. This is because more effort is needed to suppress sources of uncertainty and mitigate any problems that occur – hence the expression, 'Avoiding failure at all costs.' There is always a cost in avoiding uncertainty. However, it is also worth questioning if a project's low capacity arises from a lack of inherent value. As management experts Tom DeMarco and Timothy Lister observe, 'If a project has no risks, don't do it. Risks and benefits always go hand in hand.' (DeMarco and Lister 2003).

Establishing the capacity for uncertainty is vital because it shapes the project's strategy and permeates all the planning and management processes. This must be endorsed by the project stakeholders. If the capacity for uncertainty is high, everyone must buy-in to the possibility of failure and its consequences. Endorsement of a high capacity strategy comes at a price – is the client really prepared to accept failure as a possible outcome? If not, the project's capacity for uncertainty may have to be set lower.

Table 2.1   A project's capacity for uncertainty is influenced by many factors

Capacity for uncertainty	Key factors
High capacity	• Playing for high stakes; the benefits accruing from success justify the high risk of failure. • The organization can accommodate failure of the project (although it remains undesirable). • Consequences of failure are bounded and typically only financial in scope (that is, lives are not at stake). • Shared recognition amongst all stakeholders of the high levels of uncertainty. • Large number of unfathomable issues anticipated. • Mature processes exist for detecting and responding to early warnings of unexpected outcomes.
Low capacity	• The risk of failure outweighs the benefits of success. • Failure has highly undesirable implications. • The consequences of failure are unbounded. • Failure extends beyond financial losses; ultimately lives may be at stake. • Quantifiable uncertainty (that is, known unknowns) will predominate. • Project organization is not agile or unable to adapt to unexpected outcomes.

ACCOMMODATING UNCERTAINTY IN THE PROJECT PLAN

Field Marshal Helmuth von Moltke's famous statement, 'No plan survives contact with the enemy,' sits at the heart of any strategy for managing uncertainty. Many project plans are based on a static view of the world, fixed in time at the start of the project. Consequently, the plan only remains valid as long as this model of the future holds true. The plan describes *this* team, performing *these* tasks according to *this* specification, utilizing *these* resources. But project environments rarely (if ever) remain static, and the planning assumptions change over time. Therefore, to plan for uncertainty means a willingness to revise the plan when the situation demands.

Earlier, we identified a guiding principle that said uncertainty was an attribute of each and every element of the plan, not an item in the task list to be dealt with separately. It means that we can't treat the management of uncertainty independently from the rest of the project planning activities; managing uncertainty has to be an integral part of the planning process itself. This is at odds with the 'two step' approach which some project managers mistakenly adopt:

- Step 1: Define and manage against a nominal plan (based on a forecast of future events).
- Step 2: Use risk management to 'protect' the nominal plan.

Step 1 in effect says, 'plan on the basis that the project proceeds according to our model of how future events will unfold.' It then falls to step 2 to ensure that this model comes to fruition. But it isn't hard to see the flaws in this approach. Everything depends on the accuracy of the model and its ability to accurately predict future events given the complex and often chaotic project environment. The nominal plan is thus only an approximation (or best guess) of what will happen and remains fixed instead of evolving in response to actual events.

One of the dangers of a naively applied risk management approach is concentrating only on where uncertainties will arise and neutralizing them at source in the hope that this will keep the modelled view of the world intact. Problems occur if these risks are considered in isolation or the project manager is unwilling to concede changes to the nominal plan. Risk management can be used to protect the nominal plan, but only up to certain limits. There may come a point where the nature of the uncertainties suggest that the plan itself must evolve. Failure to recognize this will leave the project working to an outdated world-view, reactive rather than proactive.

Sailing the right compass bearing to reach port won't help if we discover a rip current is dragging us sideways. This is an example of the nominal plan being superseded by real events. Instead, we have to steer further into the current to compensate – in other words, be willing to adapt the nominal plan if the circumstances dictate it.

The different aspects of planning

Another problem is the failure to recognize the need for different types of plan. This goes beyond the usual high/low level breakdown of planning detail. When considering uncertainty, the project manager needs to think in terms of the following:

- *The baseline plan* – the commercial or contractual plan; a statement of the project's objectives in terms of milestones and deliverables. This is typically an assertion of what *must* be done, rather than an informed analysis of what can be achieved.
- *The nominal plan* – the plan which theoretically describes what we expect to happen if our forecasting model is entirely accurate.
- *The representational plan* – the plan which incorporates the chosen strategies for dealing with uncertainties. In many respects, this plan represents what is most likely to occur. It needs constant updating in response to ever-changing threats.

Isn't it unnecessarily complicated to have three different types of plan? It needn't be since these don't need to be physically separate documents. Depending on the tools available to the project manager, a single project plan can contain baseline, nominal and representational planning information. The key thing is to be able extract information relating to each of the three types of plan and know when and how to interpret this information.

The baseline plan

The project manager typically has little opportunity to influence the baseline plan, which is often agreed long before the project manager is brought on board. It summarizes challenges: essentially, find a way to deliver these benefits by these dates.

Changing the baseline plan is always difficult, and frequently impossible. In a commercial environment, milestone dates will be referenced in contracts and penalty clauses may be applied if they are missed. This makes it hard (although not necessarily impossible) to reorient the project, particularly if it is not clear to all stakeholders that the alternative is failure.

It should be remembered that the baseline plan is primarily a statement of the project objectives. Elements of the baseline plan are often formulated well in advance of the detailed analysis which determines what is actually achievable. Therefore, a project manager would be unwise to rely on the baseline plan as a working plan.

The nominal plan

The nominal plan is an idealized statement of what will happen on the project. By following the nominal plan, assuming nothing unexpected occurs and that the forecast of future events is accurate, the project's objectives will be achieved. The astute project manager may well insert some slack into the nominal plan to provide manoeuvring space should tasks take a little longer than planned, but in essence the nominal plan can be defined thus:

> *Nominal Plan: the minimum set of tasks, efficiently executed in accordance with the forecast model, required to achieve the objectives of the anticipated delivery scenario.*

This definition contains two important points:

1. Minimum set of tasks – we don't include tasks that 'might be needed' or that 'could be done.' What is the point? Every project works to a tight schedule and budgetary constraints. Effort that 'might' be needed – for instance, in

the event of an unexpected event – is handled separately, for example via a contingency plan.

2. Anticipated delivery scenario – the nominal plan is based on the assumption that unexpected events are avoided, usually as a consequence of effective risk management. By definition, only expected events are factored into the plan. Everything else is left to our strategies for managing uncertainty to deal with.

The nominal plan equates to the most optimistic outcome. It generally doesn't factor in more than a basic level of contingency against uncertainty. Consequently, nominal plans are useful for goal-setting. Project teams can (and should) be incentivized to achieve the targets in the nominal plan. Although achievable, it must be remembered that there is a strong likelihood of unexpected problems arising. Nevertheless, this shouldn't stop the team from aiming high, providing there is openness and honesty in dealing with uncertainties which are not explicitly part of the nominal plan.

The representational plan

The representational plan lies at the heart of managing uncertainty. It is the tool the project manager lives with day by day. Whereas the nominal plan says what could happen (assuming nothing unexpected occurs), the representational plan states what probably will happen, and how this will be dealt with.

The project manager will be constantly updating the representational plan with actual progress, and staying alert for deviations which could signal emerging problems. Near-term aspects of the plan may be subject to frequent revision – a fine-tuning process to adjust to continuously changing circumstances. It may well be a plan which is kept close to the project manager's chest since it will often contain unpalatable truths which may not be ready (yet) for exposure to a wider audience beyond the project team.

Why the need to distinguish between these different types of plan? Doesn't this give rise to more potential confusion? Some of the worst management errors are committed when the fundamental differences between baseline, nominal and representational plans are forgotten:

- Exclusive focus on the baseline plan: the asserted delivery dates in the baseline plan override what is actually achievable. No one challenges their feasibility until much too late in the project. It results in project stakeholders deluding themselves that unachievable goals can be met.
- The team relax into working towards the goals predicted by the representational plan, instead of striving for the milestones in the nominal plan. Any seasoned manager knows that if contingency is released at the

start of a project, it will always be consumed by the end. By setting their sights low, the chances of the team improving on the representational plan are vanishingly small.

- Without the representational plan, there is no accurate forecast of project status or estimated completion dates. The baseline plan says what must be achieved, the nominal plan says what could be achieved, but only the representational plan says what is the most likely outcome. Accurate progress reporting can only be made against the representational plan.

QUANTIFYING, DISCUSSING AND COMMUNICATING UNCERTAINTY

It is vital to have a way of quantifying and communicating uncertainty to the project stakeholders which doesn't involve arm-waving or making wild guesses. Most types of project governance will expect the project manager to account for progress, explain current and anticipated difficulties and forecast key milestone dates. But all these things are subject to uncertainty. How is the project manager supposed to discuss such awkward issues truthfully without sounding like someone who is not in control of their project?

A trap for the unwary is providing a precise answer where there is inherent uncertainty. This is usually done in the belief that the client is looking for the project manager to exude confidence and demonstrate a firm touch, tolerating no deviation from the baseline plan. All this does though, is perpetuate the misconception that all areas of uncertainty are under control. (And if this were true, there wouldn't be any uncertainty!)

The uncertainty diagram

How should a project manager answer the question: When will it be ready? It is very tempting to consult the current plan and simply read off the forecast date. The plan contains the latest and best source of information, after all.

But which plan? Not the nominal plan because that only tells us when we will hit the milestone if nothing unexpected happens. And certainly not the baseline plan because that is just an aspirational plan. So what about the representational plan which contains the most realistic forecast? The trouble with the representational plan is that it constantly changes as we address various uncertainties. Today's forecast date is unlikely to be tomorrow's. To give today's forecast date as the answer is to suggest that no more unexpected events will occur; that the forecast in the representational plan will not change again.

Perhaps we should tell the client the earliest possible date the milestone can be achieved? Or the worst-case scenario? The most likely date (but by whose reckoning)? The date which we have a 50 per cent chance of meeting?

In fact, no single date will suffice. Each is valid in its own way, but none tells the full story. The beauty of an uncertainty diagram is that it contains all of this information, and more. As a tool for communicating the inherent uncertainty in a given situation it is unparalleled because it allows the recipient to interpret the data in a way that best suits their needs.

An example may help to illustrate. Suppose the first stage of the project is forecast to be completed in 80 elapsed working days. This is a nominal-plan estimate based on the following:

- It assumes that the project manager's assessment of future scenarios is correct (that is, the plan captures everything that needs to be done).
- The planning estimates are reasonably accurate (for example, the duration of each sub-task is known with reasonable precision or slack has been added to allow for estimation errors).
- No unexpected events materialize during the course of the project.

Of course, uncertainty could change any of the assumptions listed above. (What if the plan is missing key tasks? What if there are systematic errors in the estimation process? What if something unforeseen happens?) If the unexpected outcomes are problematical, the milestone date may slip to the right. Or there may be savings: some of the tasks may be completed faster than expected, bringing the milestone date forward.

So the project manager does some further analysis, summarized in Table 2.2. Four new scenarios are identified, each of which is broken down in detail and assessed in terms of impact (that is, extra days of slippage or gain) and the likelihood (or probability) of the scenario occurring. The most likely variation arising from each scenario is the product of these two quantities:

probability of scenario occurring × impact (for example,
number of days slippage) = variation

This is exactly the process we follow in risk analysis. The only difference is that a whole set of risks have been aggregated into one scenario. For example, there are many possible risks which could lead to the failure of the supply chain but for the moment, we are less interested in the source (that is, risk) than in the outcome (the scenario).

Table 2.2   Analysing the variation associated with four possible scenarios

Scenarios	Likelihood of scenario occurring (*probability*)	Impact	Variation (*elapsed days*)
Scenario A *(supply chain fails; products are sourced from elsewhere)*.	33%	12 days slip	4 days
Scenario B *(further refinements to the specification are requested by the client once the early prototypes have been reviewed)*.	75%	24 days slip	18 days
Scenario C *(the underlying technology is flawed forcing a complete redesign of the technical approach)*.	37.5%	32 days slip	12 days
Scenario D *(testing throws up minor defects in the deliverables)*.	50%	12 days slip	6 days
		Most likely variation	40 days

We can now plot the results of this analysis on an uncertainty diagram. (See Figure 2.4).

The diagram shows four key features:

1. The earliest possible delivery date marks the left-hand extreme of the curve. Although delivery on this date is possible, the curve tells us that the likelihood is near-zero. This is the situation only if none of the uncertainty scenarios occur.
2. The latest possible delivery date marks the other extreme of the curve. Even if every conceivable scenario were to occur, the project would still be capable of delivering by this date. In effect, we are saying the project cannot fail to deliver by the 'worst case' date. If all four scenarios come to pass, the worst possible impact is another 80 days to deliver, that is, the milestone will be met after 160 days.
3. The most likely delivery date is calculated by adding together the expected variation arising from each scenario (the probability multiplied by the impact). This adds on another 40 days to the earliest possible delivery window.
4. The median interpretation of the delivery date is the point where the cumulative probability is 50 per cent, that is, where there are equal areas under the relative probability curve on either side of this date.

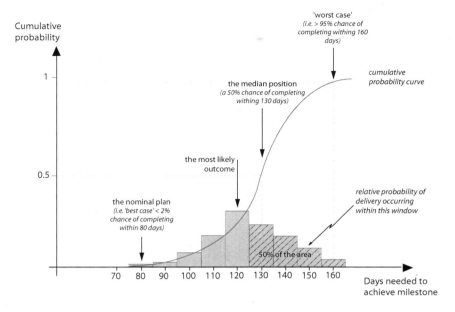

Figure 2.4   **The uncertainty diagram.** *A concise and informative way of expressing uncertainty, particularly in relation to a project's delivery schedule.*

Using this diagram to answer the client's question has several benefits:

- It lets the client draw out the information that best reflects their needs: perhaps an interest in knowing the worst that can happen, or the latest date which is 75 per cent certain to be achieved, etc.
- It re-emphasizes (in case emphasis is needed) that very little about a project can ever be absolutely certain, no matter how much is riding on it, or how much pressure is applied to the project manager.
- It clearly demonstrates the skill and professionalism of the project manager in analysing and quantifying inherently uncertain situations.
- The project manager is not making promises which are subsequently broken, for example, confidently stating a date which then cannot be achieved.

If the project has a low capacity for uncertainty, it is likely that the client or project board will be looking for a high probability completion date. (So steer the client towards dates at the right-hand end of the curve.) This still doesn't preclude the project from finishing earlier – if the project is fortunate, there may be fewer unexpected outcomes – but the chances are smaller.

The uncertainty diagram also illustrates the dangers of publicizing dates in the nominal plan. Many nominal plans tend to show the most optimistic outcomes for the project. Yet the nominal plan's completion date will only be the finishing date if nothing untoward happens in the meantime. Plotted on an uncertainty diagram, nominal plan dates tend to lie close to the left-hand end of the curve where the probability of achieving this outcome is very close to zero.

CHAPTER 3

PROBLEM-SOLVING STRATEGIES
FOR MANAGING UNCERTAINTY

It is not possible to solve a problem using the same thinking that created it.
— Albert Einstein, theoretical physicist.

CONFRONTATION MODES

Previous chapters have identified a number of factors which influence a project's approach to uncertainty:

- **novelty** – projects which venture into new territory face greater unknown challenges.
- **complexity** – large numbers of co-dependent tasks or events introduce greater potential for uncertainty.
- **affordability** – the cost of managing uncertainty has to be balanced against the threat. It may be uneconomic to tackle some areas of uncertainty.
- **structure** – the organization of the project into tasks and the choice of delivery approach determine how uncertainty develops through different project stages.
- **capacity** – projects have a higher capacity for uncertainty if the consequences of failure are judged to be acceptable. For this to be justified, the rewards of success must also be high. High capacity projects gamble that the benefits of success are worth the considerable uncertainties that must be overcome.

Taking these factors into account, a project manager must then decide how best to confront uncertainty. For example, a risk averse project with a low capacity for uncertainty will focus on suppressing as many sources of uncertainty as possible. But it will also need to be responsive to new threats and find ways to avoid or detour around these unknowns.

Figure 3.1 shows four possible modes for confronting uncertainty.

1. *Suppress* – take pre-emptive steps to reduce overall levels of uncertainty before problems occur.
2. *Adapt* – try to contain uncertainty to acceptable levels, deal with unexpected outcomes as they arise, and remain focused on the objectives.
3. *Detour* – find an alternative way to reach the objectives which avoids the uncertainty. By following a different path, any unexpected outcomes that do arise are either irrelevant or have less impact on the project.
4. *Reorient* – if unavoidable uncertainty means the project goals are unlikely to be achieved, find acceptable alternatives (or compromise).

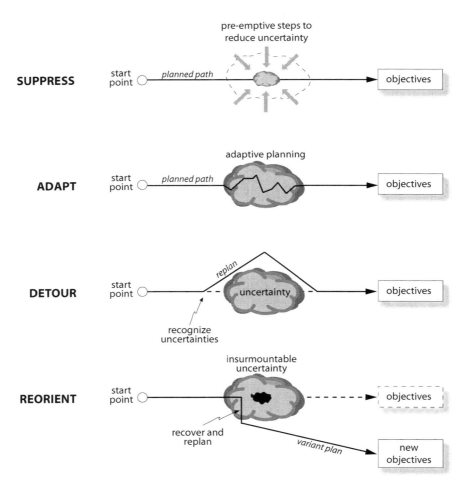

Figure 3.1   Four possible modes for confronting uncertainty

Suppression

A strategy of suppressing uncertainty is the most commonly adopted of the four modes. Pre-emptive tactics reduce the uncertainty at source, leaving the project to proceed smoothly against the optimal plan. Avoiding uncertainty by suppressing it sounds like a safe bet – and it is, providing it can be done cost-effectively. However, for novel or highly complex projects, particularly those with many co-dependencies, it may be too difficult or costly to suppress all possible areas of uncertainty.

Adaptation

By *adapting*, a project manager tolerates a working level of uncertainty but is prepared to act swiftly to limit the most damaging aspects of any unexpected events. This is a highly pragmatic approach. It requires agile and flexible management processes which can firstly detect emerging issues in their infancy and secondly, deal with them swiftly and decisively. For example, imagine a yacht sailing in strong winds. The helmsman cannot predict the strength of sudden gusts or the direction in which the boat will be deflected, but by making frequent and rapid tiller adjustments, the boat continues to travel in an approximately straight line towards its destination.

Detouring

Given the choice, we should like to *detour* around all areas of uncertainty. Avoiding the source of uncertainty means that the consequences (that is, the unexpected outcomes) are no longer relevant to the project. Thus there is no need to take costly precautions to resolve unknowns or deal with their repercussions.

Unfortunately, detouring around uncertainty is hard to achieve, for two reasons. Firstly, many sources of uncertainty are simply unavoidable, or the avoidance measures are too costly. Consider the earlier example of a subcontractor who may be incapable of delivering a critical input on time. We could detour around this uncertainty by dismissing the subcontractor in favour of a competitor who can provide a better service. This will mean cancelling existing contracts, researching the marketplace and renegotiating commercial terms with an alternative supplier – all time-consuming and potentially costly activities – and with the risk of being no better off with the alternative supplier.

Secondly, detouring only works for quantifiable uncertainty (the 'known unknowns'). Unfathomable issues often loom up out of the mist of uncertainty too fast to permit a detour.

Reorientation

Our final option is *reorientation*. This is a more dramatic form of detour where we aim for a modified set of objectives in the face of insurmountable uncertainty. Highly novel projects sometimes require this. To plough on in the face of extreme uncertainty risks total failure. The only alternative is to redefine the goals, that is, reorient the project in a way that negates the worst of the uncertainty.

This is not a tactic for the faint-hearted. Convincing the client that a project cannot be delivered as originally conceived is no easy task. But it is worth asking the question, 'Is it better to deliver something different (but equivalent), than nothing at all?'

Table 3.1   More than one way to deal with uncertainty

Confrontation mode	Implications for the project
Suppression	Uncertainty is removed or reduced by tackling its root causes. By converting vague assumptions and poorly understood issues into tangible, measurable problems, management processes can take these factors into account. This means: • identifying the sources of uncertainty; • accurately forecast future scenarios; • analysing potential threats; • converting any area of uncertainty into one or more specific problems; • developing a tactical plan to resolve the problems.
Adaptation	A certain level of uncertainty is tolerated, typically because there are insufficient resources to suppress it, or such actions would prove too costly. The threat is contained by closely monitoring key uncertainties and reacting to early warning signs. This means: • having good information-gathering and early warning systems in place; • understanding (and prioritizing) the key objectives in order to stay focused on the right things if the plan has to change; • acting rapidly and decisively; • continually steering the project towards its goals.

Table 3.1   *Concluded*

Detour	Is there an alternative path to the same objectives? This may not be the optimal route planned at the start of the project, but becomes viable once major uncertainties are identified. Be careful about avoiding one set of uncertainties only to replace them with different ones. This means: • reaching a clear understanding of the project objectives which is shared by all stakeholders; • being creative in identifying planning options; • evaluating and comparing the risks and benefits of alternative approaches; • seizing the initiative when better opportunities present themselves.
Reorient	Does the level of uncertainty represent too great a risk? Redefining the objectives may appear to be the case of thinking the unthinkable, particularly if they are written into commercial agreements. However, faced with the choice between project failure or successfully delivering against alternative goals is a viable option. This means: • understanding the nature of the threat (for example, being realistic if confronting insurmountable uncertainty); • being honest about chances of success and failure; • keeping an open mind on redefining objectives; • being persuasive in seeking the agreement of stakeholders to reorient the project.

EXPOSING THE UNDERLYING PROBLEMS CAUSED BY UNCERTAINTY

Problem-solving lies at the heart of an effective management strategy, no matter which confrontation mode is chosen. If we opt to suppress or detour around uncertainty, the problems are centred around forecasting: it is necessary to understand which areas of the project are most vulnerable in order to focus on suppressing or avoiding the appropriate areas of uncertainty. An adaption strategy means using problem-solving skills to deal with unexpected events as they occur, and reorientation is a special case where the problems are severe enough to consider redefining the goals. In all of these situations, problem-solving is a vital tool. The rest of this chapter will examine effective methods of problem-solving and look at the particular difficulties arising when many of the key variables are uncertain.

Problem-framing and problem-solving

Problem-solving breaks down into two parts. Firstly, *problem-framing* transforms a particular area of uncertainty into a set of specific problems. By so doing, we can better understand the nature and magnitude of the threat posed by the unknown. It lets us answer important questions: What are the implications of this uncertainty (that is, the range of possible outcomes)? What effect might they have on the project? Is this an acceptable risk or a show-stopper?

Common experience tells us that we can't find answers until we properly understand the question. Problem-framing is the process for doing this. We take a particular area of uncertainty (say, doubts over how a product will integrate into a client's infrastructure) and tease out the set of problems arising from this uncertainty. This means asking sensible questions and challenging any unsubstantiated assumptions: How do we find out if there are fundamental incompatibilities? What interface design methods should be used? How should we test the integration? By defining the questions that need addressing, we have taken the first step towards managing the uncertainties.

Secondly, *solution-finding* techniques provide a way to efficiently resolve the uncertainty. This means choosing from many possible solutions the one which delivers the greatest value in terms of meeting the project objectives. The solution may be to act on the source of the uncertainty (that is, find ways to effectively suppress or detour around it) or, in response to unexpected events, find an outcome which lets the project adapt to the uncertainty.

Problems and uncertainty are just two sides of the same coin: a problem is a restatement of a particular uncertainty. The point is, by taking an area of uncertainty and restating it as a problem (or set of problems) – the process of *problem-framing* – we can then apply classical problem-solving techniques to reduce the level of uncertainty.

GETTING TO THE ROOT OF UNCERTAINTY

Before we can look in detail at problem-solving techniques, there are three kinds of traps to be wary of:

1. faulty pattern recognition;
2. confusing symptomatic problems with root problems;
3. vulnerability from independent uncertainties.

Faulty pattern recognition

The human brain, although superb at pattern recognition, can be easily fooled. Because of superficial similarities, it is not uncommon to mistake a novel situation for a problem we have previously encountered. It is an instinctive reaction to ask, 'Where have I seen this before? What does this remind me of?' Drawing on experience and learning from previous successes and failures is undoubtedly a good thing, but misinterpreting a fundamentally different situation has dangerous consequences. We can end up trying to solve a different problem to the one we are actually confronted with.

Objectivity is therefore important. Ask yourself:

- What are the key *differences* between this situation and similar problems I have encountered in the past?
- Are these *significant* differences, for example, ones that act on the problem differently or at a different tempo?
- Is the scope of the problem different? Are there a larger number of variables at work?
- How timely is the previous experience? Circumstances change, methods evolve, and commonly accepted wisdom is challenged. Has your previous solution to this kind of problem become outdated?

Symptomatic and root problems

Have you ever solved a problem only to find essentially the same issue cropping up again a short while later? This typically happens when confronting a *symptomatic problem*. Symptomatic problems appear to be discrete and self-contained but actually conceal a deeper underlying problem. Because there are bigger issues at work than those under consideration, not surprisingly, any solution to a symptomatic problem tends to be ineffective or short-lived because it doesn't deal with the underlying or *root problem*.

A doctor knows that it is more effective to treat the underlying cause of illness than merely address the symptoms. The underlying illness (or root problem) can be determined by using the symptoms as clues in the diagnosis. Tackling project uncertainty requires the same approach: the symptoms of uncertainty hold the clues. Why is this task running behind schedule? There could be many root causes: lack of resources, a poorly skilled team, unforeseen dependencies or perhaps poor planning and estimation.

When we get involved in the details of framing the problems arising from uncertainty, we sometimes miss the bigger picture and mistake symptomatic problems for the root problem. By focusing too closely on gathering missing information, so much time and energy is spent on converting unknowns to knowns – through research, knowledge discovery, modelling or trial-and-error – that we lose sight of the real implications of the uncertainty.

When framing a problem it should be remembered that the nature of the parts are not always representative of the whole – for example, a collection of springs and cogwheels doesn't tell us much about how a clock functions. The root problem is not always obvious from a cursory examination of the symptomatic problems.

Breaking a problem down into smaller pieces is often seen as a good strategy, since smaller problems are easier to deal with. However, by only addressing symptomatic problems, the root problem – which lies at the heart of the uncertainty – is untouched. As Figure 3.2 shows, not all problems are fundamentally divisible. Even though each symptomatic problem has been addressed, some indivisible aspect of the root problem remains. In this case, the sum of the parts is less than the total.

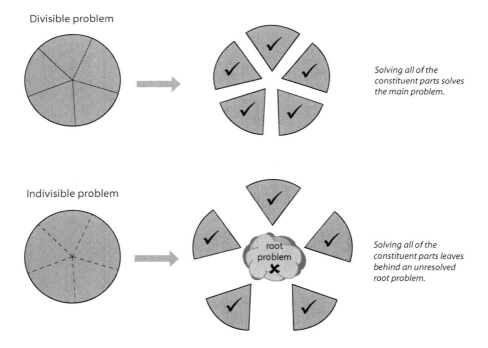

Figure 3.2   Complex problems are often more than the sum of their parts.
Breaking this kind of problem into smaller units and solving each one individually will leave behind an unresolved root problem.

Analysing the root problem

Figure 3.3 shows the steps needed to arrive at the root problem. First, collect as many symptomatic problems as possible. (A major area of uncertainty will likely give rise to quite a few.) It is important not to be too judgmental about what is relevant or important; working from preconceived ideas carries the risk of missing important implications. Avoid the temptation to filter out problems which appear unrelated; crucial dependencies or relationships can be missed.

Next, comes the step of diagnosis. Are there common themes which point to an underlying problem? Is there a pattern of association or causal links (that is, a preordained sequence or behaviour pattern)? From this diagnosis it should be possible to derive a clearer picture of the root problem at the heart of the uncertainty.

The final step is an important one: test the root problem to see if it creates the same set of observed symptoms. If not, it may not be the right root problem and a further iteration of the process is needed.

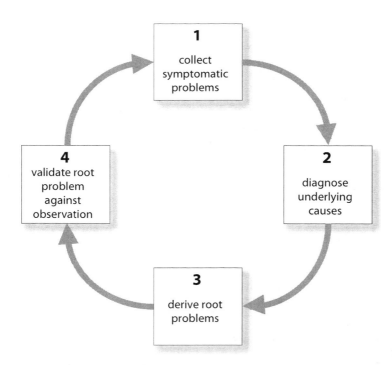

Figure 3.3   A four-step process for analysing root problems

Objectivity and insight

It is human nature to look for evidence which supports a preconceived notion and to explain away items which don't accord with the model. However, symptomatic problems which don't quite fit with the root problem should never be ignored. Objectivity is vital: a symptom at odds with the model is indicating that there are still more dimensions to the root problem to be uncovered.

Let's look at an example: At the start of a project to develop a management reporting system, the team face a key uncertainty – which database product to base the bespoke system on? A transactional database product could deliver a fast, enterprise-wide service to a large number of users but might sacrifice some reporting flexibility. On the other hand, a business intelligence product would allow users greater freedom to create ad hoc queries and slice-and-dice the data to suit their own purposes. However, the client's requirements are vague on which of these scenarios will predominate.

This one crucial uncertainty gives rise to all sorts of symptomatic problems. What trade-off should be made between speed and functionality? What size user base should be supported? What growth in data volumes should be planned for?

Table 3.2   Guidelines for framing problems arising from uncertainty

Dig deeper	Don't accept evidence of a problem at face value.
Look for the root problem	Is there a more fundamental problem which explains and summarizes a set of symptomatic problems?
Déjà vu	Many uncertainties look like something encountered before. Are these superficial similarities, in which case previous solutions may not work?
Beware of simplification	Breaking a problem down into bite-size chunks may still leave behind the root problem (see Figure 3.2).
Objectiveness	Leave behind preconceived ideas on the nature of the problem. Be guided by what the observable evidence says.
Mutually exclusive, collectively exhaustive (MECE)	The global consultancy firm McKinsey coined the acronym MECE (Rasiel 1998) to check that the facts describing a problem are mutually exclusive, (that is, each fact is stated only once, without duplication) and collectively exhaustive (that is, all the pertinent issues have been considered with equal thoroughness). This is vital for successful problem-framing.
Test the problem statement	Does the root problem account for all the observed evidence? (If not, more work is needed.)

It is conceivable that each of these problems can be systematically addressed and the inherent uncertainty reduced to manageable levels, resulting in a set of design decisions which represent the best possible compromise. But this misses the root problem. *Why isn't the client able to provide firm requirements?* Is it possible that the client doesn't really know what is needed? If true, the solution may be to implement none of the possible database solutions – what the client needs is more analysis or a period of prototyping to enable the requirements to be further developed.

Vulnerability from independent uncertainties

Launching a new drug onto the market typically costs around €750m and takes 12 years of exhaustive clinical trials before its efficacy and safety can be established beyond reasonable doubt. Collectively, pharmaceutical and biotechnology firms annually invest in the region of €70b in research and development. Much of the cost comes from conducting extensive trials which are designed not only to verify the drug's effectiveness, but to detect complications if different drugs are taken in combination, or where side-effects may be caused by certain environmental factors. Unfortunately, problems can still occur and a surprising number of drugs are withdrawn on safety grounds, despite receiving full approval for clinical use.

This is a classic example of vulnerability arising from independent uncertainties. What happens is that unconnected events combine in unforeseen ways to expose a latent flaw or weakness in the system. Individually, each area of uncertainty is small and inconsequential; it is only when circumstances cause these elements to interact in an unlikely way, that a major problem arises.

James Reason, Professor Emeritus (and formerly Professor of Psychology) at the University of Manchester, has studied this phenomenon extensively (Reason 2000). His 'Swiss cheese' model shows how this kind of uncertainty can lead to a major failure. Any complex undertaking such as a large-scale project or the introduction of a new drug has built-in barriers to guard against certain types of failure. These are the safety procedures, good working practices and proven management processes developed over the years to avoid preventable problems. However, these barriers are peppered with tiny holes (like a Swiss cheese) arising from the little uncertainties that can never be totally eliminated: the risks we haven't foreseen, the variables we hadn't considered, etc. Normally, these don't matter too much. These uncertainties fall within acceptable tolerances, and if one defensive barrier is breached, there are other lines of defence.

But suppose the holes in each successive barrier just happen to line up? The chance alignment of a whole series of minor uncertainties suddenly combines to cause a major (and potentially disastrous) outcome.

The difficulty is, there is no underlying root problem to be discovered. Our only chance of detecting such a vulnerability is to work back from a disaster scenario and identify the circumstances (no matter how unlikely) which could give rise to it. By understanding the causal factors, we can identify which areas of uncertainty require attention.

This is not unlike brainstorming around how to achieve the project's objectives, except the aim is to identify (and then avoid) *negative* project outcomes. It requires 'backward thinking' – starting with an end result (in this case, a highly undesirable one) and thinking backwards to identify the conditions which must exist to create it. We will explore this further in the *anticipation strategies* of Chapter 5.

FRAMING THE UNDERLYING PROBLEM

The main benefit of framing a problem is that it provides a structured way of gathering missing information and, equally importantly, of discovering fresh unknowns. The act of framing a problem drives us to develop a sound understanding of all sorts of different aspects of the underlying uncertainty: how far it extends, what implications arise from it, how quickly the situation is likely to change – in fact, all the characteristics of uncertainty we have already identified. It may require some kind of representational model to be built so that different aspects of the problem can be examined in different scenarios.

It enables us to approach uncertainty from a different angle. Instead of beginning with one or more sources of uncertainty and attempting to suppress or adapt to them, we work outwards from the centre of the problem. By discovering the root problem, we determine which key uncertainties must first be tackled. Going through the steps of problem-framing often reveals uncertainties we didn't know existed and is an important way of moving 'unknown unknowns' across into the 'known unknowns' quadrant.

Problems often aren't what they seem at first sight, particularly when information is incomplete. Their implications may be more far-reaching than we realize or have an impact that is felt in an unexpected way. We therefore need a formal method of formulating and evaluating the possible solutions. One such approach is shown in Figure 3.4.

The essence of framing the problem is to capture as much information as possible about the following components:

- controllable variables;
- uncontrolled variables;
- constraints acting on the variables;

- relationships between variables;
- evaluation criteria (that is, things which determine what a successful solution looks like).

Imagine the following problem scenario. Whilst driving along a minor road, a motorist comes up behind a large tractor chugging slowly along. The driver is already late for a meeting and anxious not to be delayed further, but unfamiliarity with the road means the driver can't be certain if there are safe passing places ahead, whether there are short-cuts or, indeed, if it is likely the tractor will reach its destination shortly. Using this simple example, we will examine each of the problem components as an exercise in framing the problem.

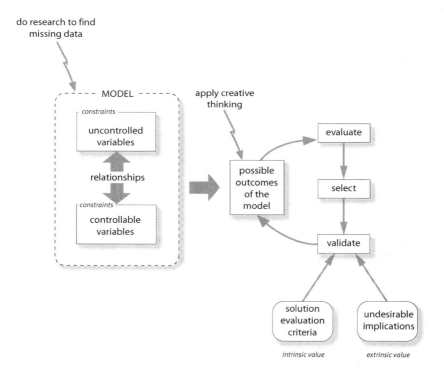

Framing the problem   **Finding the solution**

Figure 3.4   **A two-stage approach to problem-solving.** *Firstly, the nature of the core uncertainty is established by 'framing' the problem. Secondly, candidate solutions are evaluated and the one which represents the best value (within the context of the project objectives) is selected.*

Controllable variables

Controllable variables are the things which we, as the principle decision-maker, can alter or influence. In arriving at a solution, we are effectively deciding which controllable variables to adjust, and by how much. This set of variables defines our options. Although other solutions exist which aren't governed by controllable variables, these are by definition beyond our influence and therefore cannot form part of our decision-making process. In other words, we can only make decisions about things we have some element of control over.

In the example above, both the speed and direction of our vehicle are controllable. By manipulating these, one possible solution is for the driver to overtake the tractor. Another solution, arrived at by controlling the same variables in a different way, is for the driver to wait patiently behind the tractor. The most satisfactory solution will depend on the relative importance of the objectives – to make the meeting on time, or to travel safely above all else.

Just because we can identify a controllable variable doesn't mean it is relevant to the problem. We must justify why a controllable variable is worthy of consideration, or the problem will quickly become lost in a swarm of irrelevant variables. There are many other aspects of the vehicle under the driver's control (for example, the amount by which the window is wound down) but none of these have any direct bearing on the overtaking problem.

Uncontrolled variables

Uncontrolled variables include all the things that we (the decision-maker) cannot control but which nevertheless affect the possible outcomes. Some may be controlled by others who are partially within the project manager's sphere of influence, (for example, a project stakeholder). Other factors may be inherently uncontrollable.

In our example, some of the key uncontrolled variables are:

- The geography of the road. (Are there places wide enough for overtaking?)
- Forward visibility. (How far can the driver look ahead to see if it is safe to overtake?)
- The presence of oncoming traffic. (Are there gaps which would allow safe overtaking?)

Although we can't directly affect uncontrolled variables, they are still an important consideration. They define the boundary of what is within our control and what lies outside.

Constraints acting on the variables

Both types of problem variables, controllable and uncontrolled, have constraints. There are limits to the speed and manoeuvrability of the car, the width of the road, the sharpness of bends, the maximum speed of oncoming vehicles and the driver's fastest reaction time. Knowing what these constraints are fine-tunes the representational model of the problem. Within these constraints, the combination of possible values of the variables creates a set of solutions we can choose from.

Relationships between variables

Complex relationships may exist between the problem variables. For example, the greater the driver's speed, the swifter the overtaking manoeuvre but less time is available to avoid oncoming traffic, so the driver's reactions need to be quicker, etc. We also need to understand which variables have the greatest influence over the outcome. There are three main types of relationship:

1. **Strong causal relationship.** A strong causal relationship exists where there is a chain of predictable and repeatable events. ('Strong' refers to the deterministic nature of the chain of events). Strong causal relationships are comparatively rare outside of natural and scientific phenomena. A beaker of water placed in a freezer will always turn into a block of ice. Therefore, we can say there is a strong causal relationship between the initial event (water placed in a freezer) and the outcome (ice), due to the physical properties of water. The advantage of causal relationships is that if we understand the underlying principles of the relationship, we can make accurate predictions of future outcomes.

2. **Weak causal relationship.** A weak causal relationship occurs where there is only a given probability of event A leading to outcome B. For instance, there is a weak causal link between incubating an egg and a chick being hatched. B cannot happen unless A has taken place (that is, the egg won't hatch unless incubated) but the outcome (hatching) is not certain since it is possible that the egg has not been fertilized. The majority of causal relationships are weak. Our objective is to establish not only the nature of the relationship (that is, the causal chain of events) but the factors which determine the probability of each event in the chain occurring.

3. **Association.** An association exists where we can use one variable to predict the value of another, but changing the value of one variable doesn't necessarily bring about a change in the other. An oft-quoted example is the association between a person's height and their weight. We can predict with reasonable accuracy a person's weight given their height. However, it doesn't follow that reducing a person's weight will reduce their height, as might be expected if there was a causal relationship. An association enables us to predict certain aspects of variables but it won't necessarily explain

their values. Mistaking associations for causal relationships is a common problem, since the differences are often subtle. Firm evidence is needed before assuming a causal relationship.

Evaluation criteria

The evaluation criteria are a frequently overlooked aspect of problem-solving. How can we tell if we have arrived at a good solution or if we need to keep looking? It is impossible to judge unless we have a clear way of evaluating potential solutions.

As always, it is vital to keep the project objectives in mind. These provide a context for judging the value of a solution. The higher the perceived value, the more successful the solution.

In the overtaking problem, here are some possible evaluation criteria:

1. How well does it reduce the chance of being delayed?
2. Is it a safe solution?
3. Does it require more data to be gathered (for example, to consult a map for alternative routes)?
4. Does its success depend on uncontrollable variables?

Depending on the driver's objectives, different weightings might be assigned to these criteria. If a major business deal hinges on a timely arrival, criterion 1 is very important and a solution involving a bold overtaking manoeuvre may score highly. If the objective is to travel safely above all else, criterion 2 predominates. Being patient or finding an alternative route may be the optimum solution.

The fourth criterion ensures that the success of the solution doesn't depend on external (and unpredictable) factors. For example, the 'success' of overtaking on a blind bend depends on whether or not there is an oncoming vehicle which clearly isn't under the driver's control, and is therefore not an acceptable solution.

FINDING THE SOLUTION

Evaluating possible outcomes

The problem-framing process leads to a representational model of the root problem. This model enables the set of possible outcomes to be explored, each of which has an inherent value. Outcomes with a high value are desirable; these represent a good solution to the uncertainty and they accord with the project's objectives. A low value outcome is still valid, but isn't regarded as a good solution.

The value of the outcome can only be judged in relation to the project objectives. Does this solution move the project closer to its objectives? Is this a cost-effective way to address the uncertainties around which the problem has been formulated? A high value outcome will be able to answer yes to both these questions. There are usually many possible solutions, but only a very small number which deliver high value outcomes. The art of problem-solving is therefore to arrive at the 'maximum value' outcome.

In some cases it may be necessary to devise a scoring scheme so that the value of each potential solution can be quantified objectively. In fact, defining the evaluation criteria right at the start of the problem-solving process is a good idea because it demands a clear understanding of the objectives in order to get started.

Any scoring scheme needs to be kept simple. What matters most is that each potential solution is evaluated against the same criteria, and that these criteria are directly related to the project objectives.

Selecting the maximum value outcome

Once the possible outcomes have been evaluated as objectively as possible, selecting the best or *maximum value* outcome is relatively straightforward. Involving others in the evaluation/selection process can often bring a different perspective on the value of the solution. For instance, project stakeholders may have subtly different evaluation criteria arising from different vested interests in the outcome. The project manager will need to use judgment, but if nothing else, the debate will provide a useful insight into how others may react to the chosen solution.

Remember also that project stakeholders don't always share common objectives, particularly on large projects where there are diverse stakeholder interests. Consequently, what may appear to be a high value solution to the project manager, sometimes receives only lukewarm support elsewhere. In extreme cases, this leads to unexpected consequences (for example, muted support or even outright rejection) because insufficient attention was paid to the different stakeholder expectations.

Validating the solution

Before we can begin to implement a solution, two levels of validation are needed:

1. Does it achieve the objectives within the context of the framed problem? (Does it have high intrinsic value?)

2. What are the implications of adopting the solution? (Does it also have extrinsic value?)

The first of these requires assessment within the context of the problem (including all the different stakeholder perspectives). But the second needs a broader view. Are there undesirable consequences which could impact on the project objectives in a different way? If so, the end of one problem may only be the beginning of another.

Table 3.3   A primer for practical problem-solving

Beware of 'self-evident' and 'obvious'	These words often indicate variables or relationships which have been left unchallenged for too long. Challenging such assumptions may lead to better (or more) options than were originally envisaged. As a rule of thumb, the more obvious a fact, the greater the need to test its veracity.
Widen the range of the problem	Sometimes a problem is too narrowly defined and a greater range of variables needs to be considered. This can seem counter-intuitive since we are often taught to simplify and break problems into manageable chunks, but more effective solutions may appear once the scope is widened.
Non-linear causal relationships	A causal relationship is often non-linear or bounded for example, there may be a threshold above or below which the relationship breaks down. Try to understand the nature (and limitations) of the relationship in as much detail as possible.
Use creative approaches to turn uncontrollable variables into controlled ones	Some uncontrollable variables turn out to be within our control when key assumptions or established wisdom is challenged. It is worth testing the key uncontrollable variables (that is, those which have greatest influence over the outcome). It may open up a new range of possibilities.
Solve, compromise or dissolve	Some problems are intractable. No amount of effort will result in an acceptable solution and it is important to realise this before squandering vast resources on it. If no practical solution exists, consider whether there is a compromise – a 'good enough' solution, particularly if an exhaustive search for a high value outcome will be time-consuming or costly, or acceptance criteria are too imprecise to enable the set of outcomes to be properly evaluated. Finally, can the problem be dissolved by changing variables sufficiently that the problem no longer exists?

IDEALIZED OUTCOMES AND NEGATIVE OBJECTIVES

Problems formulated from uncertainty run the risk of focusing on negative objectives. How do we get rid of X? (where X represents some uncertainty). Negative objectives lead to a tendency to concentrate on symptoms (the things that we wish to avoid) and not the underlying cause, and also overlook the opportunity to design a better solution to the problem. Business consultant Roger Ackoff suggests that by framing problems against negative objectives '… we tend to walk into the future facing the past.' (Ackoff 1978).

This can lead to new problems arising from unforeseen consequences. In focusing on the thing we want to get rid of, some wider implications are missed. One example is the use of biological controls, that is, the introduction of a species to control the threat from a particular type of pest. In some cases, this has led to a much worse problem, that is, the control has become a virulent pest in its own right. In 1935, cane toads were introduced into the sugar-cane producing regions of Australia to keep down cane beetles which were eating the crops. However, the cane toad's own voracious eating habits, poisonous skin and ability to rapidly colonize, left a legacy of problems which continue today, causing major ecological damage as the cane toads own voracious eating habits.

One way of avoiding such difficulties is to refocus the problem on achieving what can be called an *idealized outcome*. An idealized outcome is an aspiration, often a restating of the project objectives. Discussions which begin with, 'If only we could …' are usually focusing on idealized outcomes. They aren't always within reach, but sometimes just the act of turning away from negative objectives and identifying idealized outcomes will suggest new possibilities.

CHAPTER 4

KNOWLEDGE-CENTRIC STRATEGIES

*No sensible decision can be made any longer without taking into account
not only the world as it is, but the world as it will be.*
    – Isaac Asimov, science writer and SF author.

USING KNOWLEDGE TO VISUALIZE THE FUTURE

Knowledge plays a central role in managing uncertainty because it enables the
project manager to model how events will unfold. Even a simple project has a
project plan – a kind of model which dictates a sequence of events, estimates
how long certain tasks will take and identifies the resources needed to accomplish
the goals. More complex projects (and especially programmes of work) explicitly
model many more key aspects of the project such as supply chain dependencies
and benefits realization.

Knowledge-centric strategies provide the ability to visualize future states of
the project. This 'forward look' is determined by knowledge of many different
variables, such as:

- What resources are needed to create the necessary outputs?
- Is it likely that the project objectives will change?
- Will external inputs be available on time?
- What levels of efficiency can the team work at?
- Are there dependencies on things outside the project manager's immediate
  control?

We can analyse different scenarios by building forecasting models of how these
key variables alter over time. The better the model, the less uncertainty there is
about the future, and the better our decision-making becomes.

Introducing the forecasting model

The accuracy of a forecasting model depends on two things, both of which are
determined by the extent and quality of project knowledge:

- *Drivers* – it is necessary to select the right variables. (that is, those that have most effect on determining project outcomes)
- *Relationships* – our understanding of how the variables behave and interact with each other.

Figure 4.1 shows how different project drivers are linked by relationships into often complex networks within a typical forecasting model. They determine the behaviour of the project (that is, how closely the project follows its plan) and therefore directly influence the project's success or failure.

We can think of each project driver as a kind of knowledge-node where a collection of facts, variables and constraints are at work. Many of these drivers are dependent on each other and even where there are no obvious dependencies, there may be subtle influences. Therefore understanding how these relationships work is another kind of knowledge.

Suppose we were planning to drive along a mountainous switchback pass. It is impossible to know in advance what dangers lie ahead, so instead we build a mental model based on experience to help predict some of the uncertainties. Because the mountainside is steep and rocky, the model tells us to be alert for

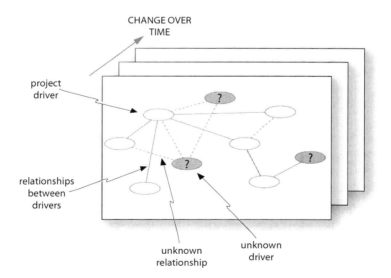

Figure 4.1   Modelling the key project drivers and their relationships. *To make accurate forecasts, it is necessary to identify the project drivers, understand how they inter-relate and how these factors will change over the duration of the project.*

rock-falls across the road. Our prior knowledge of switchback roads suggests a cautious approach to blind corners, and so on. Add in recent meteorological data and we will know whether to watch out for ice or snow on the road. The better the model, the better our chances of forecasting the unexpected and being able to deal with it effectively.

Choosing the right elements in the model

Building the forecasting model can be hard. Some of the project drivers may be hidden or their relevance only becomes apparent later in the project. Similarly, relationships may be poorly understood even when the drivers are known. Worse still, both project drivers and relationships can change during the course of the project. For the forecasting model to be useful, the project manager must have sufficient knowledge of the drivers and relationships both now and in the future.

The art of building the forecasting model is to select the right variables and ignore those that may look important but do little to influence the outcome. One way to do this is to run the model forward and examine the scenarios that emerge. Are these scenarios useful? Do they say something about the objectives of the project. If not, the model may be looking at the wrong project drivers. Only the drivers (and their relationships) which have an influence – directly or indirectly – on the project objectives are the ones that really matter.

What kind of project drivers need to be modelled? By definition they are the things which have the greatest effect on the progress of the project towards its goals. Some drivers are easy to spot while others lurk in assumptions and dependencies that may go unquestioned. (see Table 4.1.)

MAPPING WHAT WE KNOW – AND WHAT WE DON'T

Given the importance of knowledge as an input to the forecasting model, what options exist when key areas of knowledge are deficient? Suppose we can't be sure which variables or drivers are missing? This is essentially the case of unfathomable uncertainty, where we don't know what it is that we don't know. However, looking at the *boundary* of what is known can be quite informative. Organizing knowledge (that is, those things that we do know about the project) into some kind of structure, will often reveal gaps in our knowledge. Once these gaps are revealed, we have learnt something about the uncertainties. This is the first step towards converting unknown unknowns into known unknowns where risk management can take over.

Table 4.1   Identifying key drivers in the forecasting model

Key facts (which if disproved, will have a profound effect on the project).	Technology can be a key driver. Does the success of the project hinge on unproven technologies?
Variables which underpin key assumptions.	For example, does the schedule depend on achieving a quality threshold first time round?
Critical dependencies.	Are there are important activities which cannot get underway until a key task or deliverable has been completed?
Variables which may be subject to a different rate of change than expected.	Rain is forecast for the afternoon, but if the weather front moves faster than expected, the bad weather arrives in the morning. In this example, the forecast event (rain) was accurately predicted, but the timing was off.
Constants which may turn out to be variables.	The estimate of a project's completion date is sometimes based on a fixed team size. If some of that resource is taken away, it will be hard to keep to the original schedule.
Variables which sit at the centre of many causal chains.	For example, the scope of the client's requirements is a driver for estimating the resources needed, the scheduling of work, completion dates, and a range of other factors. Many different chains of causal activity depend upon this understanding of the scope, which makes it a key driver.

Knowledge maps

Knowledge maps are a practical way of addressing the unfathomable uncertainty. The process of building a knowledge map helps clarify what is known in relation to the project. By doing this, it is often possible to discover what the key areas of knowledge are and where the boundary lies between what is known and unknown.

Imagine a jigsaw puzzle lying jumbled in a box. It is impossible to know what pieces are missing just by looking in the box, that is, these are unknown unknowns. But by assembling the pieces of the puzzle, we can tell quite a lot about what is missing – the shapes of the pieces or an indication of the picture or colours gained from looking at the context of the surrounding pieces.

Building a knowledge map says nothing directly about the unknown unknowns, but it hints at where uncertainty may exist, which is valuable information in its own right. It is a way of identifying potential trouble spots in the project. Gaps in the knowledge map highlight where we need to research the nature of previously unknown problems (for example, a step towards converting unknown unknowns into known unknowns) and they indicate where we need to be extra vigilant for the early warning signs of unexpected outcomes. We will return to the concepts of *vigilance* and *mindfulness* in Chapter 7, but first we will examine some different ways of mapping project knowledge.

The domain-based knowledge map

Domain-based knowledge maps analyse different aspects of the project and quantify how much is understood about each area. At the most generic level, domains include people, infrastructure, business processes, technology, supply chains, etc. Each can then be broken down to an appropriate level of detail. To get real value out of the knowledge-mapping exercise it may be necessary to descend through several layers of detail.

Diagramming the output (as illustrated in Figure 4.2) produces an interesting visual summary of strong and weak areas. In this example, knowledge has been assessed in eight different domains. In the case of Client Requirements it has been judged that all aspects of the requirements are well-defined and this domain has been scored at 11. In contrast, the Commercial Framework domain contains key omissions and is scored at 5. Joining together the scores in each domain gives a clear visual representation of weak areas of the project where there may be considerable uncertainty. The smaller the area enclosed by the polygon (and the more distorted its shape) the bigger the problem. These are the areas to probe further.

Assessing the level of knowledge in a given domain is best done by posing a standard set of questions and scoring the response appropriately, as illustrated in Table 4.2. A more sophisticated knowledge map may apply weighting factors to important questions, although for maximum effectiveness weighting factors should ideally be determined through previously collected project metrics.

For scoring purposes, it is important to use the same set of questions for each domain otherwise a bias is introduced in the overall map. The more extensive the questions, the better, but ultimately these must be guided by the project manager's judgment. A typical set might include the following:

- What is the balance between facts and assumptions for this domain?
- Is there good breadth of knowledge?
- Is there good depth of knowledge?
- Are there multiple sources of knowledge (for example, people, documents, databases) or single sources?

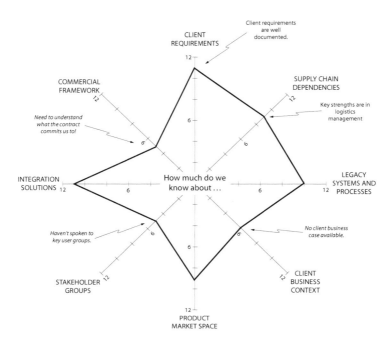

Figure 4.2   An annotated knowledge map. *In this example, a scoring system has been used to assess knowledge 'completeness' in each of eight separate domains. Low scoring (i.e. shrunken) regions indicate likely areas of high uncertainty which are worthy of further attention.*

Table 4.2   Scoring the level of knowledge in a particular aspect of the project

Score	Level of knowledge
0–2	No factual basis or experience on which to proceed.
2–4	Basic level of factual information. Information resources available but not yet exploited. Very little prior knowledge.
4–6	Factual coverage is patchy. Some of the key influencing factors are known. Some relevant experience or expertise.
6–8	Factual coverage is good but there are uncertainties over key project drivers. Good domain expertise.
8–10	Good awareness of driving factors and some understanding of the relationships and dependencies.
10–12	Detailed understanding of key drivers. Strong prior knowledge. Detailed previous experience.

- Are the sources reliable, contemporary, verifiable, etc.?
- Is there prior experience (both directly and indirectly relevant)?
- What are the immediate implications of knowledge gaps?
- What are the long-term implications of knowledge gaps?
- How well understood are connections, relationships and dependencies between key knowledge areas?
- How confident are you that the risks are understood and documented?
- Is your knowledge of this domain changing rapidly?

As this set of questions is being addressed, it is important to look for emerging patterns. Are there hot-spots of missing knowledge? Do these signify a particular weakness in the planning approach or project methodology? What is behind any significant knowledge gaps? (For example, lack of awareness, lack of source information or prior experience.) It is worth keeping a note of thoughts and ideas which occur during the mapping process – these can provide valuable insights into particular uncertainties and, with further investigation, may allow unfathomables to be 'discovered.' Once revealed, existing risk management and problem-framing techniques can be used to tame the uncertainty.

Almost any kind of modelling activity serves a dual purpose as a knowledge-mapping exercise. In Chapter 5 we will look at different techniques for anticipating future events. These different modelling techniques all provide opportunities for discovering gaps in project knowledge. It is worth remembering that as these forecasting models are built, areas of uncertainty are inevitably discovered. The astute project manager will take note of these and be alert for patterns which indicate systematic gaps in knowledge.

WHAT IS PROJECT KNOWLEDGE?

We have talked in general terms about the absence of knowledge giving rise to uncertainty, but it is time to look more closely at what comprises knowledge and how it is used in decision-making.

Uncertainty is much more than an absence of facts; it is fundamentally a gap in knowledge which may comprise many different elements. At one end of the knowledge scale is a fact: a verifiable truth about some item, event or observation which is usually quite narrow in scope. A single fact on its own may be quite worthless, but when combined with other facts each placed in their proper context, valuable information emerges. At the other end of the scale are less tangible objects: wisdom, judgment, understanding, experience. These are built on a foundation of facts and information but may be brought together in such subtle ways that even the person possessing the knowledge can't be certain how he knows what he knows. Whereas facts can easily be demonstrated to have an evidential basis (that is, can be proved or disproved), knowledge often cannot.

Knowledge is typically presented as a many-layered hierarchy (see Figure 4.3). The higher we rise through the hierarchy, the less tangible knowledge becomes. It is easy to represent and manipulate facts (for example, as computers do by converting all information – both data and commands – into a binary code of ones and zeroes). To manipulate knowledge in the same way within a computer requires far more sophisticated programming methods, such as heuristical algorithms and artificial intelligence. However, it is useful to keep in mind a hierarchical model whereby knowledge held by the individual or the organization is (a) structurally complex and (b) more than the sum of its parts.

The key aspect of this kind of hierarchical knowledge model is the difference between explicit and tacit knowledge. Explicit knowledge can be documented, stored, transferred and manipulated. We can categorize explicit knowledge quite easily which makes it relatively straightforward to build a knowledge map and see where the gaps are. But at the explicit end of the scale, this kind of knowledge is of low value. It is tacit knowledge where real benefits emerge – the wisdom, experience and know-how that may take years to be assembled. This is what enables a senior salesman to know exactly when and how to close a deal, or lets the concert pianist perform a solo recital.

Knowledge management experts Davenport and Prusak call this 'data that makes a difference' (Davenport and Prusak 1998). The problem is that tacit knowledge is hard to handle. Tacit knowledge can't always be written down or explained. A pianist who has devoted many hours to learning how to play a particular sonata still cannot explain or transfer that knowledge directly to a novice player. Some knowledge is entirely intuitive and exists only inside that person's head.

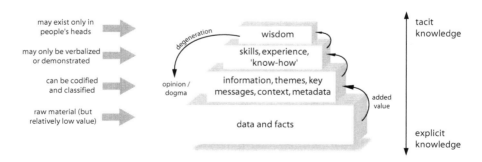

Figure 4.3   Knowledge as a hierarchy. *Gaps in knowledge often indicate more than just an absence of facts.*

For our purposes, a precise definition of knowledge is less important than the understanding that gaps at any level in the knowledge hierarchy will indicate uncertainty. Of course, a gap in explicit knowledge is both easier to identify and to remedy, for example, by carrying out factual research. Gaps in tacit knowledge are less apparent and harder to fix. Then too, tacit knowledge often has a 'shelf life' and needs constant renewal as fresh ideas and information become available. If tacit knowledge is not constantly challenged, it can wither into opinion and dogma – no use to a project manager who needs to base important decisions on currrent knowledge.

OPTIMIZING DECISION-MAKING

Having looked at what the boundaries of our project knowledge can reveal of hidden uncertainties, we have yet to explore what benefits arise from that knowledge. Knowing what we don't know is obviously of value, but how is this knowledge put to use? The answer is to be found in a project's decision-making processes.

Effective decision-making lies at the heart of managing uncertainty. If we are unable (or unwilling) to make effective decisions, then our options shrink to a single path – to let uncertainty run its course and hope that it remains quiescent. (Technically, this isn't management of uncertainty, it is abdication of responsibility.)

What kinds of decisions are needed? There are strategic decisions, for example: to invest in researching a particular area of uncertainty, or to develop mitigation plans for major scenarios, or to redefine objectives to avoid problem areas. There are also tactical decisions: how often should the team meet to discuss progress against the plan? Can this productivity trend be ignored?

Consciously deciding *not* to do some of these things is a kind of action, too – for example, when it is judged that the likelihood of a scenario occurring is too low to justify contingency planning. As the old adage says:

> *Decisions without actions are pointless. Actions without decisions are reckless.*

Taking action is just the flip-side of decision-making. Before we can act, we must decide what action to take. A professional project manager already knows how to translate decisions into actions: by communicating, delegating, reviewing progress, etc. The hard part is reaching the right decision, and doing this in a sufficiently timely fashion for the actions to be effective. Of course, if we wait long enough, it becomes easy to spot the right decision – but only because we have missed the chance to take effective action. This is the benefit of hindsight

– although the lessons can be learned for next time, that doesn't help with the immediate problem.

So if we are going to manage uncertainty effectively, making and implementing effective decisions is a fundamental part of the process. What are the hallmarks of good decision-making? Table 4.3 captures some important aspects.

Table 4.3   The hallmarks of effective decision-making

Timeliness	This is more than just the ability to make a quick decision. It is important to make the decision at the right time. A hasty decision may be regretted later, and a decision delayed for too long loses its effectiveness. Judgment is needed to decide at what point a decision will have greatest impact. A decision acts like a lever on the project: a little effort applied at exactly the right point can shift large problems out of the way.
Whose decision is it?	When an unexpected situation occurs, there is often confusion over who is responsible for making the decisions. Uncertainty over roles and conflicting viewpoints can lead to decision-making paralysis while the source of uncertainty continues to build into a crisis. It is always worthwhile clarifying decision-making roles in advance. There are at least four different levels of involvement in any decision: those who are responsible, accountable, consulted, and informed.
Involving the right people in decision-making	Simple decisions can be made (and often executed) by one person. Complicated decisions may need to be referred to a committee or project board. It is very important to involve the right people in the decision-making process and to be clear on everyone's role in the process.
Communication	The right people need to be informed about key decisions. It is important this information is effectively communicated. Project staff and other stakeholders (and particularly those charged with carrying out specific actions) need to be clear on the implications of a decision, and understand the reasoning behind it.
Consistency	When a previous situation recurs, it is logical to expect a similar decision to be made. Consistent decision-making generally leads to more predictable outcomes. The exception is where lessons have been learned and there is clear evidence that repeating an earlier decision will not lead to an effective outcome.

Table 4.3   *Concluded*

Finding the window of opportunity	Hasty decision-making can be as disastrous as prevarication. Every decision has a window of opportunity, that is, an optimum time period in which to act. Can you defer a decision without worsening the situation? By delaying you may be able to gather better inputs to the decision-making process. Conversely, if you act quickly, can you prevent an unexpected outcome from escalating into a crisis?
Measuring effectiveness	Projects are naturally forward-looking, particularly when working under pressure. This makes it hard to reflect on the effectiveness of past decisions and quantify their success. However, this is a valuable exercise. Lessons can only be learnt by understanding how decisions have influenced events. In a rapidly changing (and therefore highly uncertain) environment, this may be the key to keeping awkward situations under control.

Letting the right person decide

Decision-makers are often empowered on the basis of an existing hierarchy of authority. On some projects this may mean only a few key individuals are entrusted with decision-making powers, based on seniority or role. It can lead to all but the most trivial of project decisions resting with the project manager. Whilst this isn't necessarily wrong, in reality decisions need to be made by those best-placed and best equipped with the appropriate knowledge. This means having the right level of understanding, information, technical competence and authorization to act. This may not always align to the way a project is structured.

For instance, a senior manager may not have the right background to make important technical decisions, unlike an engineer with specialized knowledge. However, that same engineer may not have the breadth of understanding of the project to replan a delivery date; this is the manager's area of expertise. It is all a question of letting the right individual make the decision.

When unexpected events happen, they can overtake normal decision-making roles. Suppose a junior member of the team notices smoke seeping out from the door to the computer room. Everyone else has gone home for the evening. The junior might be entitled to say, 'The computer room is the responsibility of the IT manager and not my concern. In any case, I'm not the fire-warden for this floor.' However, we would like to think that the junior acts with initiative and raises the alarm, even though it falls outside their normal duties.

In many cases, swift decision-making on the part of someone not formally charged with that responsibility can avert a much bigger problem. This requires a sense of collective ownership amongst the project team, a sense of personal responsibility, and an awareness of when things are deviating from normal.

Teams which are able to respond well in a crisis tend to exhibit the following behaviour:

- a flexible approach rather than rigid decision-making hierarchies;
- delegation of decision-making to where the expertise lies;
- empowerment to override the decision-making hierarchy if circumstances demand it;
- a sense of trust and personal responsibility at all levels in the team;
- a shared awareness of what represents a threat to the project.

Evidence-based decision-making

Even when the project is optimally structured, bad decision-making habits are often prevalent. Too many decisions are based on:

- obsolete knowledge;
- personal behaviour patterns (that is, tried-and-tested approaches which have outlived their usefulness);
- strategies which work well in one context but don't translate into different circumstances;
- unsubstantiated experiences of others (that is, hearsay);
- biased information sources (for example, someone with a vested interest in a particular point of view or outcome);
- dangerous half-truths.

Uncertain situations tend to magnify these problems and give rise to particular challenges where conventional wisdom doesn't apply. Researchers such as Pfeffer and Sutton have proposed a more rigorous model called *evidence-based decision making* (Pfeffer and Sutton 2006). This forces the project to make decisions based on the reality of the situation, not preconceptions which often turn out to be wrong.

Evidence-based decision-making means:

- a mindset which is not wedded to the conventional approach;
- an ability to discard conventional wisdom if reliable evidence suggests otherwise;
- demanding evidence before committing to a decision;
- using experiments to generate evidence and test the validity of predictive models;

- rewarding decision-making based on evidence, even if the decision turns out to be wrong;
- looking for opportunities to build an evidence base to feed decision-making processes;
- continually looking for evidence to support underlying assumptions.

We can apply a simple test to any decision to see if it is evidence-based. Firstly, we write down all the evidence a decision is based on. (A blank sheet of paper at this point indicates the first stumbling block: are we making the decision on the basis of instinct or perhaps 'doing what we always do?') Then we examine where that evidence comes from. Is it evidence that already exists (for example, market reports, metrics gathered on a previous project, etc.?) in which case we must examine how this applies to current circumstances. Was this evidence gathered in a similar setting to the one we now face? If not, what aspects of the evidence (if any) still apply?

Have we gathered our own evidence? Is it possible that the gathering process has influenced the results? Most people tend to gravitate towards looking for evidence to support their pre-conceived ideas. What steps can be taken to independently verify the collected evidence?

Has sufficient evidence been gathered? Suppose a key supplier has struggled to deliver sufficient volumes of a product on two previous occasions. Switching to another reputable supplier would seem to be a sensible decision. But what if a world-wide shortage of raw materials is at the root of the problem? We will be no better off with a new supplier and possibly worse, if the relationship is untested. It is impossible to make the right decision without first gathering more evidence (that is, expanding knowledge of the marketplace).

Finally, the causal connections between the evidence and the proposed action needs to be examined. It can be difficult to be sure that the relationship is fully understood. This can lead to situations of faulty logic, of which there are many different kinds – see, for example, Jamie Whyte's excellent book *Bad Thoughts: A Guide to Clear Thinking* (Whyte 2003). It is rare to be able to make decisions solely on the basis of impartial evidence, but that shouldn't prevent a project manager from trying.

Suppose the last time I drove my car, it broke down. It broke down because the oil pressure was low. This time, I check the oil pressure before setting off and it is normal. Therefore, I won't break down. This is clearly faulty logic, showing a fundamental misunderstanding of the causal links between key variables.

Before making a decision, we must be sure to draw the right implications from the evidence gathered.

CHAPTER 5

ANTICIPATION STRATEGIES

Prediction is very difficult, especially about the future.
– Niels Bohr, theoretical and quantum physicist.

The ability to forecast how key aspects of a project will develop over time is one of the project manager's most important skills. It provides a way to anticipate vulnerabilities, that is, where and when uncertainty may upset the project plan. By anticipating problems, they can be dealt with more effectively.

Many anticipation strategies rely on modelling future behaviour and outcomes at key stages of the project. Chapter 4 first explored the idea of a forecasting model in terms of project drivers and relationships; now we will look at some different approaches to forecasting.

Traditionally, forecasting is associated with 'forward thinking' strategies which extrapolate from current events to arrive at some future scenario. But backward thinking – understanding the causes which lead to a given scenario – is just as valuable. In this chapter, we will examine ways to build forecasting models which can use both forward- and backward-looking modes of thought.

LIMITS TO FORECASTING APPROACHES

Any kind of anticipation strategy must overcome three fundamental challenges:

1. Difficulties in predicting the future state of the project, that is, where the forecasting model is incomplete or poorly understood or the quality of inputs fed into the model is poor. No forecasting model can ever be 100 per cent reliable. Any model we build is vulnerable to its own uncertainties; it can only be as good as the knowledge of the project context allows. So the less we know and understand about the project, the less effective the forecasting model.

2. Inability to identify the most likely of many possible future states. Even if the forecasting model is sound, it can be hard to identify the most likely

outcome. Why? There may be too many scenarios to analyse, or we may be faced with a continuum of possibilities that blur into each other. Although we understand the many different paths the project could take, we cannot identify the most probable one.

3. Limits on the accuracy of the forecasting model curtail its usefulness. In this case the forecasting model only provides clarity for a short distance into the future before the 'fog' of uncertainty closes in. This conflicts with the need to make far-reaching decisions right now while the future remains uncertain. Whilst we may have the knowledge which supports short-term planning, the forecasting model is unable to help with long-term plans.

It is important to acknowledge that all forecasting models are limited. If these limitations cannot be overcome (as might be the case in a highly novel project or a complex, multi-faceted programme) an alternative strategy is needed, such as *multiple explorations*. Multiple explorations don't try to model the future and they don't make assumptions about future scenarios. As the name suggests, the strategy is designed to explore different options (and reveal the problems likely to be encountered) through a series of mini-experiments. Exploration generates knowledge about the hidden uncertainties which, in the case of unknown unknowns, it may be impossible to gather any other way. Before we look at this in detail, we will first address the more common anticipation strategies.

THINKING FORWARDS, THINKING BACKWARDS

Forward thinking is a way to build a path into the future, extrapolating from what we know today to reveal something about how tomorrow may turn out. Forward thinking helps us proceed step by step towards the project objectives, analysing the risks and uncertainty along the way, identifying decision points and defining the intermediate states the project must achieve before the ultimate goal is reached. Forward thinking, at its simplest, enables the project manager to see the possibilities and choose the most advantageous.

Thinking forwards is a so-called 'left-brain' analytical activity, governed by objectivity and dispassionate modes of thought. There are many parallels with the knowledge-centric approaches described in Chapter 4. It typically includes:

- gathering information (both contextual and experiential);
- evaluating relevance and priority;
- assessing accuracy;
- combining data to create knowledge;
- modelling key project drivers and their relationships;
- determining probabilistic outcomes.

In contrast, thinking backwards helps us understand where we have come from. It lets us examine the basis for past decisions and judge if these have been effective. It too requires certain analytical abilities to understand the true dynamics of the situation, but it also requires the softer, 'right-brain' skills such as:

- intuition;
- imagining and evaluating future scenarios;
- pattern-finding (often with the benefit of hindsight);
- understanding cause and effect.

Complementary skills

Forward- and backward-thinking are complementary skills. A project manager needs to be able to switch effortlessly from forward thinking to backward thinking as the situation demands. Thinking forwards is most often associated with analysing future scenarios generated by a forecasting model. It is used to answer questions such as:

- *What are the possible futures for the project?* Knowing these allows the project manager to set targets, both interim and final. It is necessary to comprehend the full range of possibilities in order to choose the path which will lead to the desired outcome.
- *Which of these is most likely to occur (and why)?* Building a forecasting model provides a way of tackling the fundamental uncertainty concerning which of the many possible outcomes will arise.
- *What are the influencing factors and decision points (that is, causal relationships and associations) which determine the project's path?* By using the model to identify decision points, the project manager can shape the direction the project takes more effectively.

However, forward thinking is often thwarted by the sheer weight of uncertainty. Too many unknowns get in the way of understanding future scenarios clearly enough. This is where backward thinking can help, by providing vital inputs to the forward thinking processes. It leads to a clearer understanding of how the present state of the project has come about.

Backward thinking is also how we learn important lessons. If an interim review milestone has slipped by four weeks, we need to understand why. If we don't get to the bottom of the uncertainties that have caused this delay, how can we be sure that the same uncertainties won't plague the next milestone? Starting with the outcome (that is, the delayed milestone), we need to work backwards to understand each of the contributing factors – the faulty assumptions, misunderstood factors, poor estimates, etc.

At the end of a project, once all the data have been collected, backward thinking is vital for understanding where the deviations from the plan occurred and their causes. The causal relationships need to be unpicked: *this* happened because of *that* uncertainty. It is the basis for improving estimates next time round.

Backward thinking need not be limited to analysing past events. An important part of anticipation is the ability to make an intuitive leap forwards and picture a number of end-game scenarios – both successes and failures. By thinking backwards from these scenarios, it is possible to piece together the conditions (that is, events, decisions and external factors) which inexorably lead to each scenario. Recognizing the positive drivers and avoiding the negative ones greatly informs our decision-making as the project approaches these branching points. In essence, we visualize where we want the project to be and work backwards to understand which are the key decisions that will lead us there.

BUILDING THE FORECASTING MODEL

Let us examine how the forecasting model is put together in more detail. By modelling a project's most important factors – the task relationships, key variables, dependencies, resources, timescales, etc. – the groundwork is laid for exploring what happens when we vary these drivers. The model determines both the likelihood and implications of a range of scenarios. It lets us play the 'What if?' game and then prepare for the consequences.

A good forecasting model must not only identify these project drivers but properly understand them as well. What is the nature of the influence, how strong is it, when does it happen, etc.? This is the *state-driven* part of the model.

Once the model has been set up, we can run it forwards to understand something about the project's possible future states. These must be evaluated for their desirability – which of the possible outcomes will achieve the project objectives? Usually, there will be a sequence of states which lead with certain inevitability towards a final outcome, like stepping stones.

Next, we add decision-points to the model. These are the points of leverage where the project can be steered towards the objectives. Without informed decision-making, the project manager is not in control as the project rushes headlong into uncertainty.

It follows that the forecasting model must include the following:

- things that influence the project (both controllable and uncontrollable, from the project manager's perspective);

- desirable project states (that is, stepping stones to the project objectives);
- decision points.

Rapid branching

Figure 5.1 illustrates the problem of complexity faced by all forecasting models. Suppose we look ahead one month and try to understand where things will be on the project. Depending on how rapidly the possibilities branch out, it may be that there are just too many potential outcomes to evaluate objectively.

One way to limit the complexity of multiple branching is to analyse a particular subset of tasks, picking the branch (or branches) which are likely to have the greatest influence. For instance, any outcome which affects tasks on the *critical path* will be important. Since the critical path determines which tasks can directly trigger a slip in the project's end date (that is, those where there is no margin for error), focusing on these events gives more leverage in achieving a successful outcome.

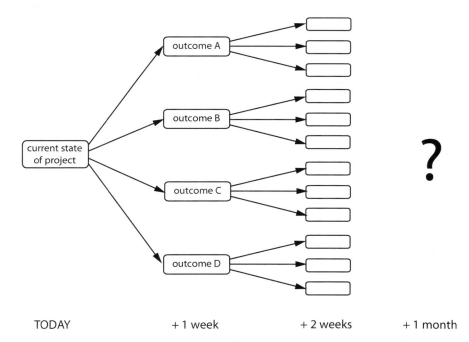

TODAY   + 1 week   + 2 weeks   + 1 month

Figure 5.1   The state-driven forecasting model. *Its weakness is that complexity can rapidly lead to many possible future states. Evaluating all the possible outcomes is too big a task without a way of simplifying the model.*

It is also possible to group outcomes, recognizing them as different aspects of an underlying root problem (see Chapter 3), which reduces the number of states left to deal with. This is shown in Figure 5.2.

In the following sections, we will look at a couple of techniques for building a forecasting model and how these provide a basis for more informed decision-making.

Decision trees

Decision trees focus attention on the *turning points* in a project, the points at which key decisions must be made. The quality of these decisions affects which state the project enters next; a step-by-step process which ultimately determines the success or failure of the project.

If the right decision is made at the right time, the project proceeds to a desired state. If not, the project begins to deviate from the desired path, although there may still be time to recover. In extreme cases, a decision may push the project into a failure state from which recovery is impossible.

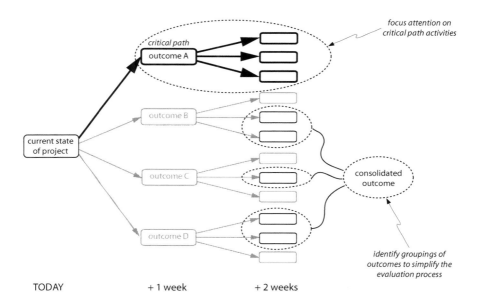

Figure 5.2   Reducing the complexity of the forecasting model. *By focusing on critical outcomes and grouping those with similar characteristics, the complexity of a rapidly branching model is reduced to more manageable levels.*

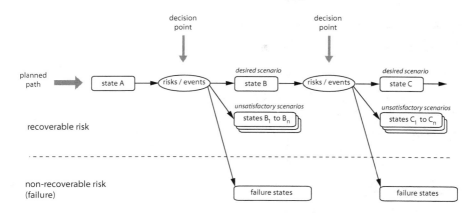

Figure 5.3   A decision tree. *Decisions taken by the project manager drive the project from one state to the next.*

The benefit of a decision tree is that it forces the project manager to identify the key project decisions. Once these have been established, the influencing factors and the raft of information needed to support the decision-making process can be identified. Attention is focused on areas which have the most direct impact on the project.

Thinking about the sequence of decision points also helps to prioritize which areas of uncertainty to tackle first. With each step, these activities reveal more about what is known and unknown, continually adding to the knowledge map. Identifying 'failure states' also warns of particularly serious risks which deserve greater attention.

A further benefit is the different perspective afforded by a decision-oriented approach. Instead of thinking about project threats in isolation, the project manager's attention is focused on:

- Which decisions are the critical ones?
- What factors affect or influence each decision?
- What are the consequences of such a decision (for example, what future states will the project enter?)

This is different to the way risks are often managed within a typical risk register. Generally, individual risks are described in terms of: a statement of the risk, its likelihood, the impact or severity if it occurs, and some consideration of countermeasures or contingency planning. The risk register focuses on describing each individual threat to the fullest extent, but risks are rarely cross-linked. Owing to the large number of potential risks, the risk register can quickly grow to an overwhelming (and largely unmanageable) size. Although this kind of risk register enables risks to be quantified and tracked in relatively sophisticated ways, its principal drawback is that the associations between risks and project states are missing or poorly defined.

A decision tree focuses attention on what the project needs (that is, the right decision at the right time) and then considers what things threaten this decision. We may end up with a subset of the same risks drawn from the risk register, but these risks have been placed into a more relevant context which means more holistic contingency plans can be drawn up.

Fishbone diagrams and backward thinking

As we have seen, forward-thinking strategies can suffer from an accumulation of uncertainty. The project manager's model builds up a picture of the future step by step. Errors, inaccuracies and missing information have a cumulative effect which, sooner or later, render the model ineffective.

This is where backward thinking comes in. By taking an intuitive leap forward (for example, imagining a future state) we can work backwards and understand what pieces need to be in place for this outcome to occur. It can be used in both a positive sense (to find the success criteria needed to achieve the objectives) and a negative one (what do the preconditions for failure look like?)

A *fishbone diagram* provides a means of capturing this backward thinking process (see Figure 5.4). Starting with the outcome on the right, the spine traces a path back in time to a known starting point. Each major branch describes a contributing factor – an event or state or decision that is needed in order for the outcome to be achieved. Ideally, these branches are arranged in time sequence, left to right. Each contributing factor is then broken down to a further level of detail, that is, what are the steps needed to create this contributing factor?

How does this help? At the end of the process, the diagram shows some important information about the major causal factors for the outcome – and often a considerable level of supporting detail. Working through the process methodically often reveals previously disregarded factors and relationships. Equally importantly, it often reveals a lack of knowledge of the causal factors. These are topics for further research, particularly where we recognize the importance of a contributing factor but have no supporting level of detail. There is still work to be done to remove inherent uncertainty, but the first step in finding these answers is identifying the questions to be addressed.

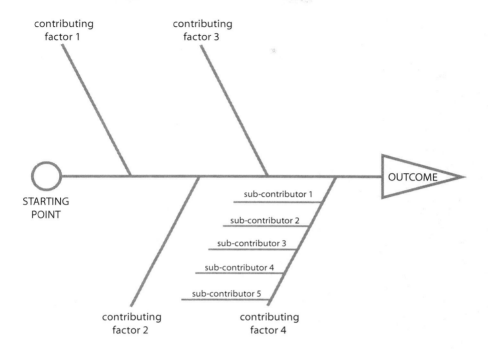

contributing factor 1

contributing factor 3

OUTCOME

STARTING POINT

sub-contributor 1

sub-contributor 2

sub-contributor 3

sub-contributor 4

sub-contributor 5

contributing factor 2

contributing factor 4

Figure 5.4   A fishbone diagram. *By thinking backwards, more is understood about the causes of an outcome. The main branches capture the key things which must be in place (or events which must occur) for the outcome to arise. Each of these can be subdivided to reveal a greater level of detail.*

WORKING WITH SCENARIOS

A drawback of model-building is that it can be an expensive, time-consuming business. It may be just too difficult, given an inherently high level of uncertainty – and a faulty model is dangerous if it leads to misinformed decisions being taken.

A useful, although less structured, alternative is *scenario-building*. Scenarios are inherently more understandable and easier to relate to. People find it easier to intellectually grasp a scenario in a way that they can't always do with an analytical model.

Whereas an analytical model is built step by step, a scenario only needs an intuitive leap to visualize a future outcome. By jumping ahead to a fully-formed scenario we are, in fact, embracing many different uncertainties simultaneously. In a typical sensitivity analysis, we look at what happens when just one aspect of the forecasting model is changed, but when we create a scenario, we change lots of variables all at once and observe the result.

Particularly for complex or novel projects, scenario-building can simplify the analysis of future outcomes. Instead of trying to assemble a mosaic out of a myriad of inputs, it allows us to jump straight to the big picture and then – by thinking backwards – work out how to get there, as shown in Figure 5.5.

Developing a scenario

Developing a scenario requires an intuitive leap into the future to visualize a particular project state, either at a key interim milestone or more likely at the conclusion of the project. It is not necessary at this stage to worry about the sequence of events that leads there; the important thing is to conceive the set of 'end-game' scenarios.

These can (and should) include both good and bad scenarios. Focusing on good scenarios helps us understand what the conditions for success will look like, through some judicious backward thinking. Bad (or undesirable) scenarios will assist in understanding what needs to be avoided and what set of contributing factors lead up to these negative outcomes.

Getting the balance right is important. Focusing too much on the positive can lead to problems being glossed over. A relentlessly positive attitude is often perceived to be a good thing, but only if allied to a fundamentally questioning and sceptical approach. Unchecked optimism can mean that the project manager doesn't work hard enough to understand where uncertainty lurks and is more likely to be caught unawares by unexpected outcomes.

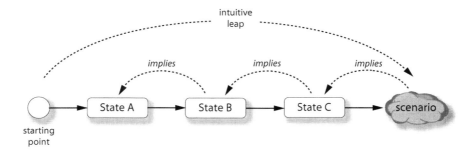

Figure 5.5   Making an intuitive leap to visualize a future scenario. *Thinking backwards identifies the key factors which need to combine to achieve the scenario. Understanding this sequence reveals where there are key uncertainties.*

Similarly, focusing exclusively on negative outcomes can lead to too much effort going into eliminating uncertainty – to the extent that the project stops moving forward and fails to take advantage of beneficial opportunities which present themselves.

Table 5.1 outlines a question-driven approach to building both types of scenario. It is best, if possible, to work through the questions in a group session with the team and stakeholders to capture as many different perspectives as possible. Normal brainstorming rules apply: encourage creativity in the first part of the session non-judgmentally and then use the second part of the session to reclassify, prioritize and evaluate the scenarios.

Techniques for explicitly changing perspective are often very helpful. One approach is to imagine the viewpoint of different project stakeholders (for example, your client, your boss, your boss's boss, an independent consultant, etc.). Edward de Bono's *Six Thinking Hats* approach (de Bono 1999) also provides a stimulating model. It requires the team to think through the scenarios together in a certain way. Everyone metaphorically dons a hat of the same colour at the same time and discusses the situation from this shared perspective (see Table 5.2). The sequence of hat colours matters less than the fact that everyone wears the same hat at the same time. For further information on this technique, Edward de Bono's book *Six Thinking Hats* is highly recommended.

Table 5.1   A question-driven approach to building scenarios

Negative-outcome scenarios	Positive-outcome scenarios
• What are your top three nightmare scenarios for how the project might end?	• In your wildest dreams, how might the project end successfully and exceed expectations?
• How could the project go wrong without it being any one person's fault?	• How could the project succeed even though some of the objectives have not been met?
• How could the project go wrong *slowly*, as opposed to catastrophically? What would be the first symptoms?	• What is the best possible outcome of the project for you personally?
• What is the worst possible disaster you, personally, can conceive of?	• Consider each group of stakeholders and imagine, in turn, what will constitute the best possible success from their perspective.
• Consider each group of stakeholders and imagine, in turn, that they will be the cause of failure. What would that disaster be?	• Which *single* aspect will dominate the successful outcome of the project: keeping to budget, timescale or quality standards?
• How could the project meet (or partially meet) its objectives and still be considered a failure?	

Table 5.2   Using the Six Thinking Hats idea to assess future scenarios

Hat colour	The team collectively discuss the problem from the perspective of ...
White	INFORMATION. The focus is on establishing what information is needed to address the uncertainty.
Red	EMOTIONS. The team considers the emotional investment of stakeholders and how this could affect the success of possible courses of action.
Yellow	OPTIMISM. For a given scenario or potential solution, the team identifies as many positive attributes as possible.
Black	PESSIMISM. Now the team takes the opposite tack and tries to find as many holes and weaknesses as possible.
Green	POSSIBILITIES. The focus is on evolving and improving the scenario to see what additional benefits can be achieved.
Blue	VALIDATION. The discussion turns to how to measure the success of the idea or, if already being implemented, to objectively review the progress being made.

Putting the scenarios to work

Having spent a little time developing a range of scenarios, it is time to put them to work. Each scenario describes a future project state: now we need some backward thinking to understand how such a state could come about. Again, a question-based approach will tease out new insights into potential areas of uncertainty, for example:

- What three questions about the scenario would you most like answered?
- What information would you need in order to be able to answer these questions?
- What actions are needed to get hold of this information?
- Imagine the future scenario is the present. What do you 'know' now that you wish you had known in the past?
- How would you have acted differently with this knowledge?
- What questions should you have asked at the time (and have you, in fact, asked them)?
- Looking 'back' what were the key project drivers?
- What were the key areas of uncertainty in hindsight?
- Was the balance of risk mitigation planning proportionate to where the risk actually lay?

Analysing the scenario can reveal a lot about the project's knowledge map. It points to what needs to be known instead of what isn't known. Not all knowledge is of equal value, so not all uncertainties need resolving. Pay attention to specific observations and any patterns which emerge: these may just hold the clues to unknown uncertainties where there is still time to act.

MULTIPLE EXPLORATIONS

The anticipation strategies discussed so far all assume that we can make some kind of limited forecast about future events, even if the details of the path ahead are unclear. Thus, we can at least see the path descending into a steep valley and climbing out the other side, even if we don't know what dangers lie in the hidden valley, be they swamps, a fast-flowing river or impenetrable thickets. The point is that we have enough information to know if we are heading in roughly the right direction. Using our knowledge and experience, we can imagine the likely scenarios of what might lie ahead and prepare accordingly for these uncertainties.

But there are some situations where this just isn't possible. We truly have so little knowledge of project drivers that it is impossible to model the project in any meaningful way. It is as if we are standing on a hillside on a very dark night. There are no lights to guide us, no clues about the terrain. Not only can we not see where the path might lead, we are not even sure there is a path. Thinking forward won't help; we have too little understanding of the situation to enable any kind of sensible analysis. Thinking backward won't help either. Even if we could imagine various scenarios, we don't understand enough about the causal chains to work back to our starting position.

This situation calls for a rather different strategy: *multiple explorations*. The idea is actually very simple. By running a number of parallel experiments (that is, explorations) each with different starting conditions or a change to a key project driver, it becomes possible to derive information about the dominant factors. A picture emerges of what works well and what doesn't. With analysis and some backward thinking, it becomes clearer why a particular exploration has been successful or not. Gradually a better understanding of the project drivers and their relationships emerges.

Furthermore, the explorations will expose any unknown unknowns – hopefully much earlier or on a smaller scale than would be case in the full scale project. Once discovered, they are no longer unfathomable and can therefore be properly taken into account in the master project plan. Such discoveries by themselves will often save the project considerable time and money, or prevent the project from failing altogether.

Each exploration is typically a subset of tasks or a rehearsal of a key part of the project. By varying just a few key factors, it is possible to see on a small scale what kind of differences these factors will make in the full scale project. This smaller investment in conducting multiple explorations pays for itself in terms of the knowledge and foresight of problems that lie ahead for the project.

In the hillside analogy, adopting the 'multiple explorations' strategy means sending off three or four scouting parties into the darkness, each travelling in different directions, radioing back reports at regular intervals about the terrain being crossed and any obstacles encountered. Not all of them will make it back (that doesn't matter!) but the group leader will develop a good idea of which directions to avoid and which offers the most promising route.

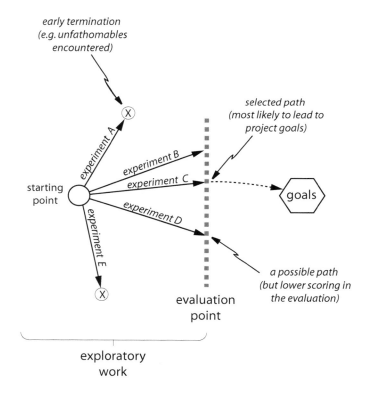

Figure 5.6   Using a multiple exploration strategy to overcome inherent uncertainty. *Each experiment adjusts one key variable. With proper analysis, failures are just as beneficial as successes because both can reveal previously hidden knowledge of project drivers and relationships.*

Objective evaluation

Many explorations will fail or fall short of a satisfactory outcome. That is only to be expected and is entirely satisfactory: the primary purpose of multiple explorations is to gain a better understanding of what drives the project towards its goals and where the threats lie, not to directly discover the optimum path to the project objectives. Failed experiments can be just as informative as more successful ones, if the trouble is taken to understand the reasons for failure.

However, it is crucial that the outcome of each exploration is objectively evaluated. This means judging how well the project objectives will be met if the exploration were continued through to the end. If this isn't done, we may end up with the illusion of progress only to find later on that we are travelling in the wrong direction. (Finding a straight and level path may enable a lot of ground to be covered but that is only progress if the path takes us in the direction we wish to travel.)

QUESTIONS OF SCALE

Scale is important when planning to use the multiple explorations strategy. It would be prohibitively expensive to set up multiple, full-scale project variants and let them run to full term to see which versions succeeded. An exploration is not the same as the actual project, and in most cases cannot be even a significant fraction of the project in terms of size, resources, timescale, etc. If such a strategy is to be feasible, the experiments must be scaled down and yet still accurately represent key elements of the project. Four factors need to be carefully considered:

1. focus on the unknown;
2. do just enough;
3. scale down;
4. consider alternative ways to 'rehearse.'

Focus on the unknown

Which aspects of a project do we *suspect* will have the most influence on its success? They might be areas known to have many risks or, alternatively, areas where very little is known and therefore likely sources of major uncertainty. Whilst it would be dangerous to rely solely on existing ideas of where there will be risk and uncertainty, these form a good starting point to create an initial set of explorations. Having conducted the initial experiments, new areas worthy of investigation may become apparent, requiring follow-up explorations.

In a manufacturing scenario, problems sometimes occur when components are brought together for integration, particularly where different suppliers or manufacturing methods are involved. Hence this would be an obvious area to target with multiple explorations: varying the order of component assembly, experimenting with different assembly techniques, working to different tolerances, etc. These explorations then need to be evaluated against clearly defined goals – for example, product quality, speed of assembly, process cost, etc.

Do just enough

How long should the experiments run? Just long enough to be able to evaluate (or in some cases, extrapolate) the outcome in terms of the project goals. An exploration also needs to run long enough to give a reasonable chance of discovering any unknown unknowns (difficult to judge, given their occurrence is entirely unpredictable). In most cases, this means that a task doesn't need to run to completion and it may be possible to start a task at an arbitrary point, perhaps using simulated inputs to gain a headstart. Since there is a cost involved with each exploration, the tasks need to be trimmed to their most essential elements without invalidating their relevance to the actual project.

Scale down

Many risky areas of a project can be scaled down in terms of both size and complexity to a much simpler model. The nature of the core problem is preserved but can now be analysed more feasibly through multiple explorations. For example, take a project which involves the connection of many tens of geographically-dispersed offices into a central hub. The essential connectivity problems may be tackled by looking at just two or three office interconnections. Investigating these issues allows the knowledge gained to be scaled up and applied to the main project. Further refinement may be added by considering other dimensions to the problem, for example, regional or international connectivity issues which can again be scaled up and incorporated into the master project plan.

Consider alternative ways to rehearse

Elements of a project selected for multiple exploration can often be explored in different ways. Instead of scaling down the tasks, we find a different perspective on the task. For process-oriented tasks, a paper rehearsal (or thought experiment) can be highly effective.

Suppose we are managing a project to develop a document management system. This system will underpin the company's business, ensuring important data such as customer correspondence is electronically captured, labelled, stored and made available to the right staff at the right time. By rehearsing the flow of information through the system using nothing more than dummy documents and a whiteboard, it quickly becomes obvious where bottlenecks can occur in the process and where there are critical points of failure in the system. At a fraction of the cost of prototyping the system, it is possible to act out (that is, rehearse) critical system functions to reveal any flaws in the logic or misguided assumptions. This extends beyond a design exercise, as it will often reveal uncertainties in roles and responsibilities and highlight where communication issues may occur. In addition, it is a good way to acclimatize staff to major organizational change. Involvement in rehearsals gets them in the right mindset, which can help to make them vigilant for emerging problems – a topic we will return to in Chapter 6.

Initiating multiple explorations

Conducting multiple explorations needs a lot of planning and organization to get the best from the strategy. What follows is a list of ideals, but some compromises may be needed depending on the circumstances of a particular project:

- If you can, establish the key areas of uncertainty first, so that the explorations can be as narrowly defined as possible.
- Vary one (and only one) key variable or driver in each exploration. If you vary more than one, you can't be sure which variable had the greatest effect on the outcome.
- Run as many parallel explorations as there are major variables.
- Keep the environment in which these explorations are running as similar as possible to avoid influencing the outcomes.
- Stop an exploration as soon as a negative outcome becomes clear – as long as you have gathered sufficient data to understand the causes of that outcome. (You may be able to reallocate resources to refining more successful explorations.)
- Establish a way of assessing the outcome of each exploration and of monitoring progress. What constitutes a positive outcome?

A 'multiple explorations' strategy is relatively uncommon in commercial project environments because of the comparatively high investment needed in time and resources. However, it is the logical way to approach highly novel projects (or large programmes) particularly where a modest upfront investment in multiple explorations has the potential to save huge sums (and embarrassment) by avoiding major uncertainty later in the programme, when plans have been authorized and resources committed.

Far more common is the idea of the pilot study or a prototyping activity, prior to undertaking the main programme of work. This 'single exploration' can reveal important information (for example, by uncovering unknown unknowns) but lacks the richness of multiple explorations because no comparison of outcomes can be made. However, that is not to dismiss the benefits of prototyping – any knowledge gained about future uncertainties is always beneficial.

CHAPTER 6

RESILIENCE STRATEGIES

In any moment of decision the best thing you can do is the right thing,
the next best thing is the wrong thing, and the worst thing you can do is
nothing.
                                    – Theodore Roosevelt, 26th President of the USA.

A large-scale project is often *monolithic* – that is, everything is invested in one project infrastructure: one way of working, one set of relationships between supplier and client, and one set of tools and processes. Similarly, big programmes generate huge momentum which makes it difficult to change direction suddenly or react to unexpected problems.

With so much invested in a large project, the planning must often stretch years into the future. The level of detail and forecasting accuracy upon which so many decisions and huge sums of money depend, creates obvious weaknesses. Unfortunately, this means a monolithic project is often built on a set of planning assumptions which are fixed and immutable, even though the plan may be forced to change for a variety of reasons. Vulnerability to uncertainty is built in – either because of inflexibility when the unexpected happens, or because latent uncertainty is unknowingly incorporated during the planning stage.

AGILITY

An *agile* project is much better able to cope with unexpected outcomes. Agility means the project can avoid surprises (that is, detour around uncertainty) by recognizing early symptoms – or once encountered, can quash the undesirable consequences. Although uncertainty is just as unwelcome to the agile project, it holds less fear for the project team who are better equipped to deal with such situations.

The opposite is true for a typical monolithic project. Once something unexpected has occurred, its consequences can be more serious and far-reaching: reaction times are slower, chains of command are longer, and it takes more effort to untangle the dependencies and understand their implications. Consequently, monolithic projects must invest heavily in uncertainty prevention measures such as risk management and contingency planning. But as we have already seen, although these measures are effective against the kinds of uncertainty we know about (the 'known unknowns') they are powerless against the unknown unknowns which won't appear in any risk analysis.

Does this mean large scale projects are forever doomed by unfathomable uncertainty? Not necessarily. Even large scale projects can operate in an agile fashion but it takes considerable effort (not to mention changes in mindset) to break away from monolithic thinking.

Becoming agile

Although large-scale projects often have inherently greater complexity and hence experience more uncertainty (see the discussion on *Project Complexity* in Chapter 1), they often have surprising flexibility for introducing agility, if done at the start of the project. Agility implies features such as:

- division of project tasks into small, self-contained components;
- decoupled dependencies wherever possible (for example, by introducing schedule 'buffer zones' or planning a fallback position);
- early warning detection of emerging problems;
- rapid response to problem indicators;
- willingness to exploit opportunities (even where this means deviating from the plan);
- putting in place responsive management processes;
- empowering the project team.

Whilst none of these steps are necessarily straightforward, empowering the project team is often the biggest stumbling block. Staff empowerment often means tearing down long-established ways of working based on the rigid hierarchies within an organization. But it is just this sort of rigidity which, through extension, leads to project bottlenecks – for example, bureaucratic ways of working with complex reporting structures, centralized (but uninformed) decision-making, and painfully slow response times. All these factors are the antithesis of agility, and making the switch to more agile ways of working can seem counter-intuitive to some senior executives.

Agility in large scale projects

Large scale public sector projects undertaken by UK Government, particularly IT-based programmes, have suffered more than their fair share of high profile failures, despite the introduction of more structured controls in recent years (for example, Gershon 1999; Cabinet Office 1999; Cabinet Office 2000).

However, observers have noted a distinct change in procurement policy on the part of UK Government: a move away from monolithic projects undertaken by a single supplier selected through competitive tendering, towards the increasing use of *supplier pools*. Here, a small group of suppliers are down-selected into a supplier pool and bid for smaller work packages via a series of mini-competitions. An otherwise monolithic programme is decomposed into discrete projects where no one supplier dominates, encouraging a better fit of skills, methods and experience – or so the theory goes. Whilst this incurs some additional overhead in managing and integrating the programme, it compartmentalizes risk within each project. It also provides an escape route for failing workstreams: projects which get into trouble can be terminated and re-bid without bringing down the entire programme.

Meeting uncertainty with agility

Recalling the confrontation modes identified in Chapter 3, once the opportunity to suppress or detour around uncertainty has passed, only two options remain: adapt or reorient. Both strategies require agility – how fast can the project adapt and cope with the unexpected, and how flexible is the project in identifying new objectives? Table 6.1 illustrates some of the key factors which determine a project's agility in the face of uncertainty.

Table 6.1   Key factors which determine the agility of a project

Taking small steps	Small steps are easier to conceptualize, plan for and manage. Small steps can be retraced more easily if they haven't delivered the required results or when it becomes clear they are leading in the wrong direction. Small steps also support the idea of *fast learning loops*. For instance, a lengthy project phase reduces the opportunity to quickly feedback lessons learned. If the project is too slow to respond, it may fail under the accumulated weight of uncertainty.
Working iteratively	A feature of monolithic projects is the assumption that everything proceeds more or less as a sequence of tasks executed on a 'right first time' basis. Generally speaking, more effort is directed at protecting this assumption (for example, by analysing and mitigating risks) than on planning for a certain level of rework. By planning to tackle tasks iteratively, two benefits are gained: firstly, early sight of unfathomable issues which wouldn't otherwise surface until much later in the schedule, and secondly, greater opportunity to make controlled changes.

Table 6.1   *Concluded*

Early warning mechanisms	Unexpected outcomes rarely happen without warning. A good early detection system is vital: frequently scanning for problems, knowing what 'normal' looks like (and thereby detecting abnormalities more easily), and spotting patterns in seemingly unconnected problems.
Willingness to change what isn't working	An agile project is continuously looking for ways to improve. A project which is unable (or unwilling) to learn lessons is destined to repeat its mistakes because it ignores opportunities to learn from the unexpected. However, continuous improvement can have repercussions beyond the project, and implementing organizational change is never easy. The appetite to learn lessons has to be present before progress can be made.

FAST LEARNING LOOPS

A fast learning loop enables a project to follow a structured approach to executing tasks and yet remain agile. There are two key ingredients in a fast learning loop. Firstly, key activities are planned to be iterative, that is, closure is only reached after two or more cycles of work have been completed. This differs markedly from sequential execution where each task is assumed to complete in a single pass (see Figure 6.1). With a fast learning loop, each task reaches successively higher stages of completion at the end of each cycle. Secondly, the frequency and rapidity of each cycle allows sufficient opportunity for the lessons of the preceding cycle to be incorporated in a timely fashion.

Since fast learning loops promote agility within the project, it is a valuable strategy for dealing with unfathomable uncertainty. Although it doesn't avoid the uncertainties altogether, it does provide an effective coping strategy.

The benefits of iteration

Those who have conducted detailed analyses of the software industry (for example, Boehm 1981) have long known that the cost of making a change increases by roughly an order of magnitude for each stage in a sequential project lifecycle. A change made early on (say in the analysis stage) leads to fewer complications – and is therefore much cheaper – than introducing the same change during testing. Similarly, fixing bugs that are revealed during testing is significantly more expensive than investing more time early on to get the design right in the first place.

SEQUENTIAL stages

ITERATIVE stages

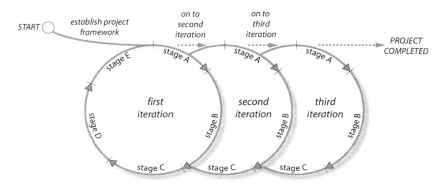

Figure 6.1   Sequential and iterative project methodologies. *Adopting an iterative approach means the completeness of each stage increases with successive iterations until the project objectives have been met. The benefits are flexibility and adaptability to uncertainty.*

A benefit of the fast learning loop concept is that it forces segments of each stage to be completed earlier in the project cycle. None of the stages are completed in the first iteration (this would make the project a sequential project, by definition) but enough is done to tease out uncertainty that might otherwise remain dormant until much later.

Finding problems early on is valuable: the earlier their detection, the less expensive the remedy, and with care, the follow-through effects are significantly reduced. In the IT industry this has been encapsulated in many different software development paradigms from the 'build a little, test a little' concept through to agile programming, extreme programming and more holistic methods such as the Dynamic Systems Development Method (DSDM Consortium 2007).

Before these iterations can begin, some preparation is needed. We must determine which of the outputs are incrementally developed in successive iterations, and create an over-arching management framework. But once the iterations are set going, outputs emerge more quickly – an important factor in dealing with the associated uncertainty.

Table 6.2   Getting the best out of iterative working

Create a framework	Iterative projects still need a road-map of where they are heading. A certain amount of planning and analysis needs to be done before the iterative cycles can begin. This work will ensure that the project objectives are kept firmly in sight.
Prioritize what needs to be achieved	The choice of short-term objectives for each iteration is key to the success of the approach. See *prioritize high value tasks* later in this chapter.
Time-boxing each cycle	Keeping to the planned schedule for each cycle is paramount. Unfinished work should be evaluated and if judged sufficiently important, carried over into the next iteration. A pattern of unfinished work across successive cycles may indicate uncertainties in the planning process which need to be addressed.
Each iteration is reversible	Sometimes it is necessary to reverse out of a blind alley. By keeping the scope of each iteration small, unpicking a cycle need not be a disaster for the project.
Empower the team	Each iteration is a turn of the wheel and to deal effectively with uncertainty, the faster the wheel turns the better. That means passing more responsibility down to team members than might normally be the case, so that decisions rest with those who are best placed to make them.

Techniques such as DSDM finesse the iterative concept by focusing each cycle on a different aspect of the project. Typically, a business case or feasibility study initially establishes the context for the project and identifies broad project objectives. A first iteration will focus on the *functional model*: identifying, creating and reviewing functional prototypes, repeated as necessary according to the complexity of the project. The outputs of this work then inform a second key iteration: *design and build*. This time design prototypes are identified, created and reviewed with the results feeding into the third major iteration of *implementation*. During a final series of iterations, operational issues such as user training and support capabilities are developed.

Iterative approaches provide a powerful way of dealing with uncertainty:

- more frequent checkpoints provide opportunities to review and fine-tune the plan based on what is observed;
- successive iterations allow the opportunity to feedback experience gained so that the project strives for continuous improvement;
- early iterations uncover unfathomable uncertainty earlier in the project lifecycle;

• mistakes uncovered in one iteration can be addressed in the next iteration.

THE SHEWHART CYCLE

The Shewhart Cycle was originally developed as a model to promote organizational change, but has been widely adopted as a strategy for dealing with all kinds of dynamic project environments. When W. Edwards Deming began examining quality control issues in the US and Europe in the 1970s and 80s (Walton and Deming 1992), the Shewhart Cycle formed the basis for systematic improvement in many different industries (and is often referred to as the Deming Cycle).

It comprises four key steps: Plan, Do, Check, Act. (See Figure 6.2) This sequence is repeated continuously throughout the project's life, with each iteration moving the project closer to its overall objectives. Its real strength lies in its formulation of a process for exerting control in a rapidly changing environment, whether that be competing effectively in the marketplace or coping with highly novel projects.

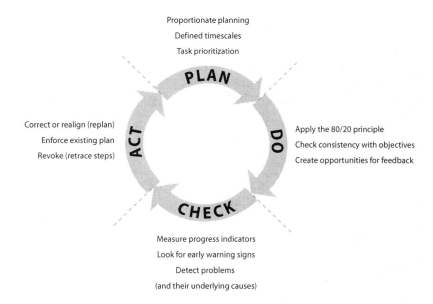

Figure 6.2   The Shewhart Cycle. *Through successive iterations, the knowledge and experience gained is incorporated into the next cycle. The speed of the cycle and the responsiveness of the project team are key success factors*

Plan

The principle of *proportionate* planning is an important feature of the Shewhart Cycle. Proportionate planning means only developing the necessary level of planning detail at the right time. A proportionate plan is also an honest plan – it is usually better to acknowledge the unknowns than to make guesses. The further ahead the plan looks, the more uncertainty there is. Developing a highly detailed long term plan is often counter-productive: it is labour intensive and can provide a false sense of security when working assumptions begin to be treated as facts over time.

Planning realism requires:

- in-depth planning detail for near-term activities (for example, the next iterative cycle);
- outline planning for the medium term (that is, the planning framework);
- strategic objectives for the long term;
- a schedule for when plans need to be revisited and more detail added.

Do

During early project cycles, the 'doing' stage will draw out unfathomable issues. This is positive in the sense that once discovered, the project manager can address these uncertainties (for example, by modifying the plan for the next iteration or by taking the appropriate mitigating action). As a result, early cycles may well not run to plan. This is to be expected, and the benefits will become apparent in the later iterations which will generally run more smoothly as a result of problems being detected and fixed early on.

The question of which tasks are done in which cycle is enormously important. (Many projects never even consider alternative sequences or give any thought to task prioritization). This is vital if the project has adopted a time-boxing approach (that is, the time allowed for each cycle is rigidly fixed, what varies is the amount of work completed). The following sections provide some guidance.

Look for problems
Do the hardest, riskiest, most uncertain tasks first – providing that their relevance and importance to the project objectives is undisputed. (If not, these activities may be 'gold-plating' and should be relegated further down the list of priorities). Confronting the hardest tasks first, flushes out major uncertainties. Bear in mind the economics of fixing issues early – this is far more cost effective than tackling unexpected outcomes in the latter stages of the project.

Prioritize high value tasks
The high value tasks are the ones which deliver maximum benefit for lowest input. It is the governing principle behind the 80/20 rule (see Figure 6.3). In many fields of activity, a large proportion of the results (say 80 per cent) can be produced with a minority of effort (say 20 per cent). (There is nothing magical about the 80:20 ratio; it is merely illustrative of the unbalanced relationship that often exists.) These are the quick wins. Conversely, completing the last 20 per cent consumes proportionately more of the effort.

Consider the process of housebuilding. The external structure goes up quickly and we immediately recognize the structure as a house. It can seem as if the project is nearly done. But the internal floors, electrical fitting, plumbing, plastering and decorating all take much longer to complete. Roughly 80 per cent of the fabric of the house is assembled in about 20 per cent of the time. But it may take a further 80 per cent of the time to complete the last 20 per cent of the work.

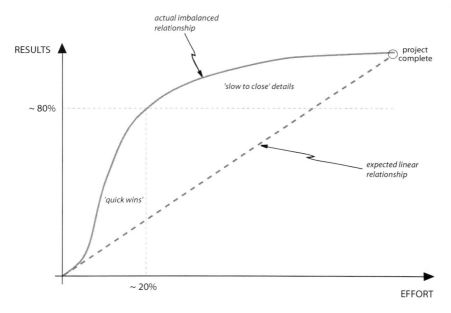

Figure 6.3   The 80/20 principle (Pareto's Law). *Many tasks have an imbalance between the effort applied and the results obtained. Often, a majority of the results can be achieved with a minority of the effort. Exploiting this leads to 'quick wins' which reveal hidden uncertainties much earlier in the project lifecycle.*

Prioritizing the 'high value' tasks will generate rapid progress on the project. From this advantageous position, it is easier to spot if any of the remaining activities can be scaled back or dropped.

Check

Checkpoints provide the opportunity to take stock and measure how well the plan is being met – both for the current cycle and the overall objectives. It is logical to have a checkpoint after a period of activity, but if the project cycles are long, too much time may have elapsed between a problem materializing and its analysis. If the project is to be truly agile, checking (at least on an informal basis) will need to take place in parallel with the *do* part of the cycle.

Unfortunately, there are many examples of projects which have sophisticated measurement and information-gathering processes which nevertheless fail to spot major problems in time. If it isn't already obvious what needs to be measured, simplicity is usually best. Consider the following:

- What are the best indicators of progress on the project?
- What are the indicators of potential failure?
- How rapidly do these indicators vary (and therefore what is the optimum rate at which to monitor these signals?)
- How quickly will you need to react? (Will the problem have transformed into something different by the time you act?)
- What are you checking against? There needs to be a yardstick for comparison which is established at the start of each iteration. Is the project meeting these expectations? Exceeding them? Falling behind? The reasons need to be understood in each case.

Act

The *act* part of the cycle is where learnt lessons are put into practice. Only by taking specific action can the project avoid making similar mistakes (or encountering similar uncertainties) in the next cycle. The project manager can choose to act in one of three ways:

1. Action to *correct or realign* the project. This is designed to return the project to its baseline plan, for example, by adding more resources if the schedule is slipping or, alternatively, reducing the scope of work. The speed of action is determined by the circumstances. Normally, these actions feed into the next iterative cycle but in a crisis the cycle itself may need to be speeded up.
2. Action to *enforce* the current plan during the next iteration. This signifies that the project remains on track or has only deviated in minor ways.

However, there is still a need for the project manager to be proactive in implementing the existing plan.

3. Action to *revoke* the current iteration. This indicates that the project has taken a wrong turn. Some or all of the work done in the previous cycle may need to be retracted and a different approach taken. A correction to the plan will not be sufficient to recover the situation so more drastic action is required.

THE NEED FOR SPEED

There are many variations of cyclical control processes like the Shewhart Cycle. One noteworthy example is the *OODA loop* which has recently gained credence in certain business management circles (for example, Richards 2004). OODA stands for Observe-Orient-Decide-Act and was the brainchild of a renowned US fighter pilot Colonel John Boyd (Coram 2004). It embodies the strategies he used to gain air superiority in a dogfight – skills that were honed during many combat missions flown in the Korean War.[1]

- Observe – gather information relevant to the problem; notice patterns and trends; be dispassionate and objective in gathering the facts (that is, go beyond merely looking to confirm preconceptions).
- Orient – place the observations of the problem in context; understand which are the dominant factors; draw on previous (but relevant) experience; filter the relevant from the irrelevant.
- Decide – choose a course of action which will reduce the threat; evaluate a range of possibilities; consider undesirable side-effects as well as the benefits.
- Act – implement the decision swiftly and with precision.

The OODA loop is intended to be a tool that will help gain advantage in a competitive situation. By cycling round the OODA loop faster, one's opponent is left disoriented and falls behind the pace. Mastering the OODA loop means taking control of a situation which can then be exploited to gain an advantage.

This may not seem relevant to managing uncertainty, but if we view uncertainty as the opponent, the benefits of the OODA loop become clearer. Instead of being forced on the defensive and having to respond to unexpected events, rapid

---

1   Boyd practised what he preached. He was nicknamed '40 second Boyd' for the standing challenge he issued to fellow pilots. Starting from a position and orientation of their choosing, he wagered them $40 that he could manoeuvre his fighter into an advantageous attack position within 40 seconds. Though many accepted his challenge, Boyd never had to pay up.

execution of the OODA loop allows the project manager to regain control over an uncertain situation – to end up driving forward a resolution instead of merely reacting to events (that is, falling behind the curve). If nothing else, Boyd's OODA loop shows the necessity to evaluate a situation and act decisively – and with sufficient rapidity – to seize back control of the situation.

SAFETY NETS

A safety net is there to catch us should we fall. If we don't fall, we may wonder why we bothered with it. In these situations, a safety net is just an encumbrance we didn't need, consuming time and effort that could have been spent elsewhere.

If a project has a high capacity for uncertainty and can afford to take a bold stance (see Chapter 2), perhaps a safety net isn't needed. As Philippe Petit, the man who famously walked a high wire between the twin towers of the World Trade Centre, pointed out, good preparation is its own kind of safety net. But if a project has nothing to fall back on, either it must be certain of its preparations or the organization must be willing to accept the possibility of failure.

Most projects do need a safety net. There is too much at stake: large investments, profit margins, careers, reputations, brand loyalty – perhaps even social welfare or health and safety issues. Most projects are created on the assumption that they will succeed – and some on the basis that they *must* succeed. In such cases, it is not a question of whether we can afford to build in a safety net; it is a question of whether we can afford not to – and in many cases the answer is that we can't.

So what safety nets are available to the project manager? Obvious measures such as mitigation planning, disaster recovery planning, and business continuity arrangements are effective responses to specific and targeted threats (providing the economics of the situation can justify the investment in these preparations). But these are largely crisis management techniques, things to be enacted once the damage has already occurred. What we are looking for is an early warning system *before* the situation begins to get out of control. For this to happen, we need to turn our attention towards *trigger points*.

TRIGGER POINTS – PREVENTING UNCERTAINTY FROM ESCALATING

We first touched on trigger points back in Chapter 1 as the moment when latent uncertainty begins to give rise to observable problems (see Figure 1.4). In fact there are two kinds of trigger point:

- an outcome which wasn't expected (a *positive* trigger);
- an expected outcome that doesn't happen when it should (a *negative* trigger).

Clearly, the earlier these outcomes are detected, the better the project's chances of dealing with the consequences. Identifying trigger points and watching for the early signs forms a kind of safety net for the project: even if all other strategies for avoiding uncertainty fail, early detection can reduce its impact.

There are few unexpected events which aren't preceded in some fashion by warning signs. Increased seismic activity forewarns of a volcanic eruption, and the ocean retreats before the onslaught of a tsunami. Similarly, uncertainty warning signs are often subtle and easily overlooked. They can be short-lived and leave little time to react. However, for a project which is vigilant and mindful of the indicators, there is a brief window of opportunity where unexpected outcomes are not yet fully formed and may still be prevented. (Chapter 7 examines the need for vigilance in more detail.)

Figure 6.4 shows a typical timeline for uncertainty. On the lefthand side, there is latent uncertainty – things with the potential to cause problems which have not yet manifested themselves. We have looked at a range of anticipation strategies designed to suppress latent uncertainty or detour around it. The righthand side shows the situation once uncertainty has developed into unexpected outcomes. Here we can use resilience strategies which enable the project to either adapt to the unexpected or, in extreme cases, reorient the project towards different goals

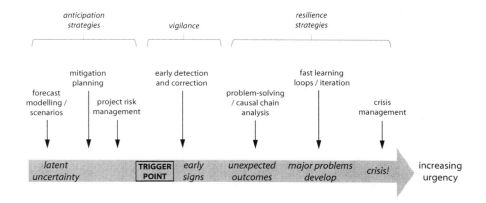

Figure 6.4   A timeline for uncertainty. *Anticipation strategies reduce the threat of uncertainty, and resilience strategies minimize its impact. In between sits a narrow window of opportunity for the vigilant project team capable of acting rapidly and decisively.*

altogether. In the middle sits a narrow window of opportunity: the transition period when something unexpected is starting to happen but events have not yet reached a level of seriousness to attract attention. Although unusual things are occurring, these are not yet obvious to the team – deviations are still below acceptable thresholds, small problems are accumulating unnoticed, etc.

Because these effects are subtle, it takes a pretty sophisticated level of vigilance to spot the warning signs. All members of the project must be equally vigilant. There is no telling where the warning signs may first arise, and certainly not enough time for normal reporting mechanisms to pass messages up through the management hierarchy.

MAINTAINING PROJECT STABILITY

A common reason for missing early warning signs is the outward appearance of stability. Often, a period of project stability is mistaken as an absence of uncertainty: for example, the team are reporting that key work packages are under control, intermediate milestones are being achieved, measures of 'burn-rate' (for example, cost, manpower, consumables, etc.) are falling within acceptable tolerances, and risks are being controlled. These are good news items, but none of these implies an absence of uncertainty.

Project stability is an illusion. In fact, a kind of dynamic tension exists between unplanned events which, if left unchecked, will draw the project away from its nominal path, and the constant corrective actions of the project team struggling to keep the project on track. This is illustrated in Figure 6.5.

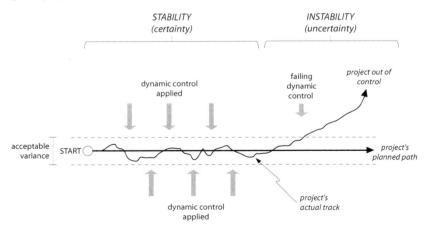

Figure 6.5   The illusion of project stability. *A dynamic balance exists between uncertainty and corrective actions which gives the illusion of stability.*

The psychologist James Reason calls this kind of stability a 'dynamic non-event' (Reason 2000). Stability only exists because there are constant adjustments being made to preserve the nominal progress of the project. Remove this constant adjustment and stability falls away rapidly.

Table 6.3 highlights the important consequences of this kind of dynamic tension for the way a project team needs to function.

Table 6.3   Spotting problems emerging out of the dynamic tension

Key attributes	Putting it into practice
Team involvement	The whole team must be involved in dynamic adjustment, not just the project manager. This means individual team members are best-placed to notice when the amplitude of the required adjustment increases (a warning sign).
Setting low 'noise levels'	There is a statistical noise level associated with the project. This is determined by the type of metrics being used to track progress, for example, number of defects appearing, individual productivity measures, number of client issues flagged, etc. For an unexpected event to become noticed, it must rise above this noise threshold. The threshold depends on a raft of factors such as project culture, feedback mechanisms, communication channels and the mindset of individuals best placed to notice the developing problems.
Acting on the unusual immediately	A culture of collective problem ownership and responsibility is important. All team members need to be capable of resolving issues within their domain as soon as they are spotted. This means normal adjustments are not referred upwards to await a time-consuming decision; they are part of the day job.
Minimizing the thresholds of acceptable deviation	Project tolerances set by the project manager can sometimes mask the beginnings of a problem. Thresholds need to be set low enough so that issues are picked up earlier, giving more time to react effectively.
Operational awareness	The first symptoms of problems usually come from the operational side of the project, that is, those at the sharp end who are closely involved with the core project activities. A project manager can easily become distanced from these activities, reliant on second-hand information such as progress reports, diagnostics and performance metrics. Team members are always an important source of information. It should be remembered that their concerns about progress are not always voiced through formal channels.

CHAPTER 7

LEARNING STRATEGIES

Every failure teaches a man something, if he will learn.
— Charles Dickens, *Little Dorrit.*

LEARNING TO IMPROVE

Getting better at dealing with uncertainty – whether by learning from mistakes, or consciously and continually looking for ways to improve – is partly a question of developing the right mindset. Many organizations never really learn to deal more effectively with uncertainty because they lack a strong enough desire to improve. There are plenty of excuses: no time or budget to invest in improvement, too much pressure to deliver, no one available to lead the initiatives. Sometimes there is complacency (how can we improve, we're already so good!), or just the feeling that improvement is too difficult. To improve, the *desire to improve* must be part of the mindset.

A seven-step learning strategy

Figure 7.1 outlines a particularly effective learning strategy. The sequence of seven steps follows a rolling, circular path where the lateral motion implies progress is being made, that is, lessons are being learned and applied in a way that results in measurable improvement over time. It is a never-ending sequence: since uncertainty exists on every project, there are always opportunities to improve.

1. *Receptive to learning.* Project teams and organizations can only learn lessons if they are receptive to learning. Paradoxically, one of the dangers of success is complacency and an unwillingness to acknowledge the possibility of failure. It is fine for a project manager to motivate a team by instilling belief and confidence in their abilities, but this needs to be tempered with realism. Success today is never a guarantee of success tomorrow. Many projects now operate in such cut-throat business environments that standing still (that is, failing to improve) is tantamount to falling behind rivals who are continually looking for ways to innovate and increase efficiency, thereby stealing a march on the competition.

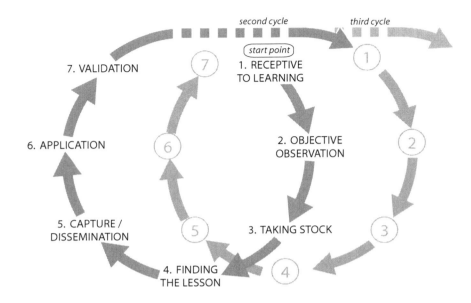

Figure 7.1   **A seven-step learning strategy.** *The time taken to complete one cycle will vary. It could be the duration of the project or there may be opportunities to complete many learning cycles in the course of a single project.*

2. *Objective observation.* A key element of any learning strategy is objectivity. Failing to observe what *really* happens when we deploy our strategies for managing uncertainty means that no lessons (or the wrong lessons) will be learned. Whilst absolute objectivity is impossible (we are, after all, part of the system being observed), it is important to remove any *perceptual filtering* that might be colouring our view of success or failure. Perceptual filtering occurs when we have an unconsciously biased view. Errors of perception happen when we only look for evidence to support preconceived ideas, and ignore data which contradict our existing model. Ideas for improvement are most likely to occur when a project can step away from its preconceptions and examine evidence of behaviour, decision-making, etc. with true objectivity. This may require the participation of independent observers who don't share the preconceptions of the project team.

3. *Taking stock.* At least once in its lifecycle, a project needs to take stock of its uncertainty management strategies. This means switching the focus away from project objectives and the normal duties of project execution and taking a considered view of how well the management processes are functioning (and specifically those which address project uncertainty). There are natural breakpoints (for example, major milestone deliveries, end of phase, end of

project) where this can be done, or the project manager may need to create artificial breakpoints. Many management methodologies (for example, PRINCE2) require a post-project review which usually takes place after the majority of the project objectives have been accomplished. The elapsed time helps achieve the objectivity needed to capture and quantify lessons. This is much harder to do when there are still major uncertainties pressing down on the project and the final outcome is not yet clear.

4. *Finding the lesson.* Some lessons are obvious, some require much soul-searching, brainstorming or independent analysis. Occasionally there is no real lesson – a project may have done everything possible to deploy effective uncertainty strategies and still not have achieved the desired results. It is not worth agonizing over such situations if there is genuinely nothing of significance to learn. Then too, it is important to remember the 80/20 principle (see Chapter 6, *Prioritize high value tasks*). Focus on learning the most valuable lessons and act on them first. A simple change may be all that is needed. This step should never descend into a needlessly bureaucratic exercise.

5. *Capture and dissemination.* Too many projects and organizations reach this stage in the learning cycle but fail to adequately capture the knowledge or pass the lessons on to the next generation of projects. Clearly, without effective capture and dissemination things won't improve for future projects. Choose an approach which best suits your organizational culture: peer group reviews, knowledge repositories, mentoring, formalized reports, project wikis, etc.

6. *Application.* Any project in its startup phase should be actively seeking out lessons from similar projects and considering how best to implement them. In many cases, this can be incorporated into early stage planning reviews:

   – Which previous projects have the closest resemblance? (This may need to be broken down according to a number of different project attributes).
   – What were the lessons learned on these projects?
   – How are these lessons being incorporated into the planning for this project?

This is a crucial step in the cycle – it is where change is implemented. It is pointless to go through the previous learning steps if the knowledge isn't going to be properly applied.

7. *Validation.* Not all lessons will deliver the expected benefits. This may be because a lesson has been misinterpreted, misapplied or isn't appropriate to the current situation. It is important to validate the effectiveness of the lesson and the underlying reason for its successful (or otherwise) application. A promising improvement or new technique may turn out to

be a one-hit wonder or a statistical anomaly – so it must be unlearned. Equally, knowledge which has brought significant benefits needs to reinforced. Validation works best where there are objective measurements of improvements (for example, through capturing and analysing project metrics).

THE CONSTRUCTIVE MINDSET FOR MANAGING UNCERTAINTY

In the final analysis, the success of any learning strategy will depend on the quality of people in the project team, and the culture or mindset which they adopt.

The people factor – organizing for success

Staffing up the project team with the right blend of people is clearly desirable, but it is not the only thing needed. The project manager must know how to organize the team for success. Barry Boehm's landmark work in the IT industry (for example, Boehm 1981) offers valuable advice which still holds true today – and not just for IT projects:

- *Better and fewer.* Don't throw people into your project team unnecessarily. Bigger teams don't mean better teams. If you choose the best people (and get the right mix), a smaller team size will be more effective in tackling uncertainty.
- *Placement.* Fit the skills, experience and aspirations of team members to the right roles in the team.
- *Offer career progression.* Let each team member see how making the project a success will benefit them at a personal and professional level.
- *Balance the team.* Pick a team for its complementary skills. Strengths and weaknesses will balance out across the team, with the right mix. A team with similar skills, experiences, attitudes and personalities may be too narrowly focused because everyone will think and act alike.
- *Cull misfits quickly.* Be alert for team members who cause problems and lose them from the project as quickly as possible.

DEVELOPING A CONSTRUCTIVE MINDSET

The mindset of the project team has a much bigger influence on the project's ability to deal with uncertainty than commonly thought. Attitudes shape perception and influence actions. Many studies have shown that the way we view an uncertain situation (for example, whether we embrace it positively with determination to succeed, or resent its problematical nature and are pessimistic about the chances of success) dramatically influences the actual outcome. Constructive attitudes are far more likely to result in constructive outcomes. In this sense, mindset is a very relevant part of the strategy for managing uncertainty.

What is a mindset exactly? It is the core set of values held by an individual. It is the attitude, perspective and frame of mind which is brought to bear on a particular problem. When the majority of individuals in a team share the same mindset, it becomes the *culture* of the project.

It has been suggested that there are six key properties which make up team culture (Schein 2004):

- sharing of basic assumptions;
- origination by the group (that is, discovered or developed internally);
- origination in response to a problem or in the face of adversity;
- acceptance that demonstrable benefits arise from adopting the cultural behaviour;
- communication of the culture to new members of the team;
- encapsulation of the 'correct' behaviour to be used in tackling problems.

When the unexpected happens, the team's shared mindset (see Figure 7.2) automatically leads to actions which tackle the uncertainty effectively. In contrast, if team members need time to decide how to respond, or whether to pass decisions up a chain of command, the advantage of decisive action is lost. Uncertainty is much harder to contain under these circumstances.

It is difficult to define all the aspects of a truly effective mindset which, in any case, needs to be adapted according to the situation, but the following points may serve as a guide:

- Be willing to confront possible areas of uncertainty without being prompted. Anticipation can curtail uncertainty before it develops into undesirable outcomes.
- Be sceptical of received wisdom. Independent, objective, evidence-based decision-making is key. Once things are labelled and categorized as facts, they often cease to be questioned.
- Regard the project plan as a guide, not a fixed map of the territory. Plans often need to change in the face of uncertainty.
- Don't lose sight of reality. Too many plans are built to fit deadlines, not the other way round.
- Encourage diversity in thinking within the team. If everyone thinks alike, you will only get one view of the problem.
- Establish open and honest communication channels. Without these, reaction times to unexpected situations are stunted.

- Encourage blame-free reporting of problems, errors and concerns.
- Instil an attitude amongst the team of worrying about failure (in a positive sense).
- To avoid unexpected outcomes, assume the worst about uncertain information. Projects which assume everything is okay unless a problem is reported, tend to suffer more failures than ones which actively establish their status regularly.
- Encourage the team to challenge decisions constructively. It is a mistake to believe those in authority always have the necessary knowledge and appropriate experience to make the right decisions.
- Demand to be told bad news in regular progress meetings. It almost always exists, unless someone is holding back. Never accept silence as confirmation that all is well.
- Find time to visualize future scenarios for the project, both good and bad.
- Be creative when considering possibilities. (See *Harnessing Creativity* later in this chapter.)

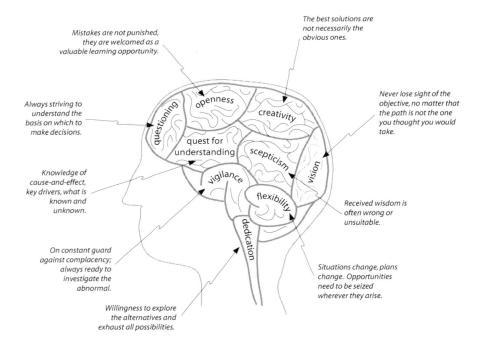

Figure 7.2   An idealized mindset for managing uncertainty.

MINDFULNESS AND VIGILANCE

In their book *Managing the Unexpected*, Weick and Sutcliffe use the term *mindfulness* to describe a state of mind which is alert to the potential for unexpected situations to arise (Weick and Sutcliffe 2001). The idea arises from their analysis of certain types of organization which face particularly difficult challenges in managing uncertainty. These organizations conduct complex operations and operate in highly unpredictable environments where the potential for error can have very serious consequences. Examples include nuclear power generation plants, aircraft carrier flight decks and fire-fighting crews. Weick and Sutcliffe call them *high reliability organizations* (HROs).

The concept of mindfulness sums up the differences in culture and management processes which are common to the HROs examined by the authors. Although the severity of these challenges are, by and large, not those faced by the typical project, the lessons are no less pertinent.

Mindfulness is a comprehensive, holistic approach to containing uncertainty in typically high risk environments. HROs have cultivated mindfulness because the alternative – eventual failure of potentially catastrophic proportions – is simply unacceptable. But mindfulness requires a fundamental change in attitude which is neither cheap nor easy to bring about. It requires a big commitment, and outside of HROs, relatively few projects play for such high stakes. But there are a number of key principles from which valuable lessons can be drawn.

Five key attributes

Weick and Sutcliffe found that successful HROs tend to share five key attributes:

1. preoccupation with failure;
2. reluctance to simplify interpretations;
3. sensitivity to operations;
4. commitment to resilience;
5. deference to expertise.

Preoccupation with failure

To find the signs of emerging unexpected events, you have to look for them. The best way to do this is to become preoccupied with failure, whether by continually worrying about the possibility of failure, being attentive to its warning signs, questioning whether there are different explanations for seemingly obvious results, or going out of one's way to investigate any anomalous outputs. Crucially, becoming preoccupied with the possibility of failure should not be seen as a negative attitude.

Organizations that exhort staff to believe the mantra 'failure is not an option' may be missing a fundamental point: uncertainty is ever-present and the very worst thing we can do is to deny its existence. Failure is very much an option for every project, and the project teams which succeed are likely to be the ones which keep this in the forefront of their minds.

Reluctance to simplify interpretations

As a project manager struggles to understand what is happening within the project, there is a natural tendency to look for evidence to support preconceived ideas and reject what doesn't fit. However, all evidence needs to be considered on its own terms.

Suppose the development of a software module has fallen a couple of days behind schedule. If the project manager has already expressed doubts about the developer's skill level before the assignment, it is easy to interpret the latest delay as confirmation of this developer's lack of experience. But is this really where the problem lies? What if the original work estimate was unrealistic? If true, then reassigning the work to a more experienced developer won't fix the problem. All it will do is delay discovery of the real issue – a potentially far more serious problem in the way project tasks have been estimated which could mean that the entire development activity has been underestimated.

Avoid reaching for the obvious explanation and thereby failing to consider viable alternatives. Simple explanations are attractive but bring with them the risk of oversimplification.

Sensitivity to operations

Early warning signs tend to be subtle; their insignificance makes them easy to overlook. Consequently, problems may lie undetected, often for some time, before their negative aspects attract attention. James Reason refers to these as *latent failures*. Even if the transition period is long, the effects of the problem are low-amplitude and difficult to notice without superb vigilance. Unless the team is sensitized and highly attuned to such anomalies, the clues are missed until the failure ceases to be latent and materializes into a full-blown problem.

Becoming sensitized to the warning signs (what Weick and Sutcliffe refer to as 'maintaining situational awareness') is difficult. It requires a change of attitude across the whole team, not just the project manager. It is resource intensive – both in terms of the efforts made to detect the warning signals, and in the resources to follow up, analyse and determine if there really is a latent failure.

It also needs a thorough understanding of what 'normal' should look like on a day-to-day basis for the project. This is the benchmark against which deviations and anomalies can be measured. In a typical HRO, even though the environment is complex (think of the many variables and control processes of a nuclear power plant, for instance), the concept of normality is well-understood. Operational outputs are well defined and anything out of the ordinary will be quickly picked up. This is less often the case for a project – particularly for novel projects where there is little or no experience on which to base expectations or even assess progress. Measuring progress against the project plan can be self-deluding, particularly if the plan itself is based on considerable uncertainty and represents only what we would *like to see* happen.

Commitment to resilience

A commitment to resilience means recognizing that any aspect of the project can be subject to uncertainty. No aspects are off-limits. All that matters is that the team is ready and willing to confront any symptoms of uncertainty as soon as they are detected. Deviations from the norm are kept small by applying work-arounds or taking swift remedial action. This damps down the tendency of the project to diverge from its planned path. It may be possible to prepare in advance, for instance by:

- building slack into the plan;
- envisioning all the different ways for the project to fail;
- building contingency plans in the event of the most likely failure scenarios;

or it may be necessary act quickly in real-time through:

- harnessing creativity and innovation to adapt to unexpected events as they occur;
- engendering a shared understanding of what personal and project-level failure looks like, and thereby being vigilant for any occurrences;
- effective communication of observed anomalies (and honest reporting of errors).

Deference to expertise

When a project goes off the rails, it is not uncommon to hear someone say, 'I knew it was coming; if someone had asked me about X, I could have told them there was a problem.' Encouraging problem ownership will ensure that individuals don't shrug their shoulders when they see a problem developing and assume that someone else will deal with it. But it also means that responsibility for dealing with problems must reside where the expertise is greatest. Under normal conditions, this is determined by the decision-making hierarchy in the project. But in times of crisis, this can become a bottleneck. For example:

- Swift action is needed to prevent an unexpected outcome developing into a crisis, but it takes time to communicate vital information up the chain to the project manager (or another stakeholder).
- The decision-maker does not automatically have the clearest understanding of the problem. Sometimes those who detect the problem have the best idea of its solution, but such information is not always communicated, or the message gets filtered out along the way.
- Confusion exists over who needs to make a decision, delaying action. Unexpected situations may not fit into predefined responsibility structures. Whose job is it to deal with a particular anomaly? In the time it takes to resolve the question of responsibility, the situation may have significantly worsened.

Where swift action is needed, the question of trust becomes important. Is the project manager prepared to trust less senior members of the team to take important decisions (for which the project manager retains responsibility)? For this to work, there must be a shared understanding throughout the team of the project objectives and the threat posed by uncertainty.

HARNESSING CREATIVITY

Having looked at a wide range of strategies for dealing with uncertainty, it is clear that these have largely been process-driven strategies. Following a process provides stability in what may otherwise be a very dynamic environment. Process-driven strategies encapsulate previous experiences of dealing with uncertainty; their rules help guide us towards taking effective action and steer clear of known pitfalls. But one of the dangers of an obsession with the process-driven view is that it drives out the freedom to be creative. As Tom DeMarco points out, 'The danger of standard process is that people will miss chances to take important shortcuts.' (DeMarco 1999). Consequently, many people fail to make the proper connection between creativity as a key ingredient of problem-solving and the non-prescriptive application of uncertainty strategies.

Creativity should be a core part of the project team's mindset. It is an important tool for breaking free from a cycle of mistakes where lessons are not really learned and management strategies stagnate. Creativity is the driving force behind change and improvement. Established wisdom – especially when confronting near-term uncertainty – can be quite limiting. Creativity offers the chance to come up with a *better* solution.

Promoting creativity

There is no prescription for creativity. To be creative often means tearing down boundaries, ignoring the rules and challenging what everyone commonly accepts as fact. The reason why creativity is important is that effective solutions are often in a different place to where the symptoms of the problem show up. It takes a certain creative insight to distinguish between the problem and its underlying concepts. Table 7.1 lists some of traits which encourage creative thinking.

Table 7.1   Mindset traits to encourage creativity

Constantly ask searching questions	Question everything – even the most obvious things, because sometimes the most obvious things are the hardest to see. Don't be satisfied with explanations which are based on accepted wisdom. What are the facts? Where is the independent evidence? We all know of examples where assumptions turn out to have been made in error. Consider bringing in an outsider who doesn't share these assumptions and take note of their view of the situation.
Play the 'what if' game	Changing one aspect of a situation can illuminate a whole range of possibilities. What if we built a prototype *before* developing the detailed design? What if one of the key requirements was removed – would it greatly speed up delivery? Chapter 5 looked at some techniques for visualizing future scenarios by playing the 'what if' game and then working back to see how these scenarios might come about.
Strive for innovation rather than incremental improvement	Radical solutions tend to arise not from refining existing approaches but by making intuitive leaps. Truly innovative solutions are more likely to offer double-digit improvement than fine-tuning an existing strategy.
Consider things from different perspectives	As we saw in Chapter 5 (*Working with Scenarios*) Edward de Bono has put forward some powerful ideas for using different perspectives (de Bono 1999). Putting on a different hat is a metaphor for analysing the problem from a particular viewpoint, one that means adopting certain attitudes which may be very different to our own stance. By wearing each different type of hat, we gain new insights on the problem.

Table 7.1   *Concluded*

Draw a picture	Restating a problem in a different medium often has the surprising effect of revealing new aspects or triggering new ideas. If the uncertainty problem is already written down (e.g. a risk captured in a risk log) draw a diagram as well. Mind-mapping is a useful technique (e.g. Buzan 1999). Explain the problem to someone who doesn't have the same background. Again, this can often be a fertile exercise in generating new insights on the uncertainty.
Don't run from failures	A failure doesn't have to be a dead-end. A failure is often a step forward in the sense that it narrows the possible options. There are countless examples where apparent failure then led on to success: the accidental secondary fermentation in a bottle of wine which led to the invention of champagne; 3M's invention of a glue which failed to be very sticky but was the basis for the Post-it note; the failure of a new drug designed to treat high blood pressure which turned out to have some interesting side-effects (Viagra).
Set time aside to reflect	Opportunities to be creative get squeezed out by the day-to-day pressures of running the project. Time needs to be set aside to specifically address project strategy: how best to deal with a major area of project uncertainty, what can be learnt from previous experience, what opportunities does this uncertainty present? The project manager needs to be able to step away from the minutiae of daily management on a regular basis in order to gain a broader, more holistic view of where the project is heading.
Set goals and fix deadlines	Part of creativity comes from challenging rules and 'thinking outside the box' but this only works when we really understand what the limits of the box are. How will we recognize an innovative approach? What are the *real* goals? (Bear in mind these may not be the goals we think they are.) Creative thinking needs to be focused on specific objectives otherwise we are unlikely to break away from traditional solutions.

FINAL THOUGHTS

We began by imagining a toolkit of techniques and methods for managing all the different aspects of uncertainty. These are not magic-bullet solutions or processes to be blindly followed, but a broad range of proven methods which, with judgment and skill, can significantly improve a project's ability to cope with uncertainty. Each chapter has looked at different aspects of that toolkit; how to use a particular strategy, when to use it, and where its particular strengths lie.

As with any job, it is a question of choosing the right tool to match the problem at hand. No two projects are ever exactly alike, and despite apparent similarities, each project faces its own unique set of uncertainties. Above all, the project manager must evaluate each new uncertainty afresh and pick from the toolkit to create the appropriate strategy.

There are no easy answers and no quick fixes when it comes to managing uncertainty. But as we have seen, there are strategies which, with some care and thought, can improve a project's chances of success. What matters is how you take these and adapt them into solutions which fit today's needs, and then evolve them to meet the challenges of tomorrow.

GLOSSARY

agile project	A project which adopts various management strategies which allows it to cope better with uncertainty.
association	An association exists where the value of one variable can infer the value of a second variable. However, a change in value does not bring about a change in value of the second variable, for example, as in the occasional association between a person's height and weight.
causal relationship – strong	Exists where there is a chain of predictable and repeatable events, for example, water turning to ice when its temperature is lowered.
causal relationship – weak	Exists where there is a non-zero probability of event A leading to outcome B.
confrontation modes	A set of different tactics for dealing with uncertainty, that is, suppression, adaption, detouring and reorientation.
critical path	A subset of sequential activities in the project plan which must be completed on time or else a key milestone will slip.
decision tree	A model of where key decision points occur in the project lifecycle and the possible outcomes that can arise from these decisions.
driver	Key aspect of a project which significantly (and disproportionately) influences progress toward the goals. These are the 'control levers' which determine the path taken by the project.

fast learning loop	A structured management approach whereby a project is able to rapidly respond to uncertainty and apply the lessons learned in later stages of the project.
fishbone diagram	A diagrammatic representation of the factors which contribute to a particular project outcome.
forecasting model	A semi-formalized view of how key project variables are related and change over time.
knowledge map	A structured record of what is known (or how much is known) about given aspects of a project. Gaps in the knowledge map are often useful pointers to key areas of uncertainty.
mindfulness	A state of mind which is alert to the potential for unexpected situations to arise.
mindset	The set of shared values and principles within the project team which supports uncertainty management strategies.
mitigation plan	A series of actions designed to avoid or reduce the detrimental effects of one or more risks.
multiple explorations	A set of experiments which reveal how key aspects of the project develop when the starting conditions are varied.
novel project	An original or highly innovative project, often attempting to reach goals which have never been achieved before.
plan – baseline	The plan containing the contractually defined milestones. This plan is often a statement of objectives and is not necessarily based on a realistic estimate of what is feasible.
plan – nominal	A feasible (but typically optimistic) plan by which the project objectives can be met. Whilst it may contain a certain level of contingency planning, it cannot fully address all aspects of uncertainty.

plan – representational	A plan maintained day-to-day recording actual progress and assessment of the most likely future outcomes. It is a snapshot of progress plus a forecast.
problem-framing	The process of formally stating the nature and scope of a problem arising from a particular area of uncertainty.
risk	An expression of a conceivable or quantifiable threat which endangers the accomplishment of one or more of the project goals.
root problem	An underlying (and sometimes concealed) problem which may give rise to a set of symptomatic problems. Solving symptomatic problems does not solve the root problem.
scenario	A visualized future state of the project. Scenarios may be bad as well as good. They act as a reference point for understanding the conditions necessary to arrive at a given scenario.
stakeholder	Anyone with a vested interest in seeing the project achieve its goals. This can include a wide range of representatives drawn from both the client and the supplier organizations.
symptomatic problem	Although appearing to be a discrete and self-contained problem, a symptomatic problem is triggered by a more fundamental root problem.
uncertainty (generically)	The sum of the unknown and unknowable aspects of the project, the consequences of which may threaten the achievement of one or more project goals. It is the intangible measure of what is not known about the project.
uncertainty – indeterminate	A type of uncertainty where the outcome is unknown and the set of possibilities is also unknown or ambiguous, for example, attempting to predict what may be written on a business card.

uncertainty – inherent	The full set of project 'unknowns' prior to identifying and analysing risks.
uncertainty – latent	The uncertainty which remains after risks have been identified. This includes 'unfathomable' issues – threats which either cannot be quantified or conceived of.
uncertainty – unfathomable	A type of uncertainty which cannot reasonably be conceived of in advance, that is, an 'unknown unknown.' This is sometimes called 'a bolt from the blue.'
uncertainty – variable	A type of uncertainty where the outcome is unknown but limited to a knowable set of possible outcomes, for example, picking a card at random from a pack of playing cards.
workflow	A sequence of tasks carried out in a logical order which minimizes the dependencies between tasks.

BIBLIOGRAPHY

Ackoff, R. L. (1978), *The Art of Problem Solving* (John Wiley & Sons).

Apgar, D. (2006), *Risk Intelligence* (Harvard Business School Press).

Bernstein, P. L. (1998), *Against the Gods: The Remarkable Story of Risk* (John Wiley & Sons).

Boehm, B. (1981), *Software Engineering Economics* (Prentice Hall).

Brooks, F. P. (1997), *The Mythical Man-Month* (Addison Wesley Longman).

Buzan, T. (1999), *The Mindmap Book* (BBC Books).

Cabinet Office (1999), *Modernising Government* (Cabinet Office).

— (2000), *Successful IT: Modernising Government in Action* (Cabinet Office).

Computer Associates (2007), *The Changing Facing of Project Management* (Loudhouse Research).

CCTA (1998), *Managing Successful Projects with PRINCE2* (The Stationery Office).

— (1999), *Managing Successful Programmes* (The Stationery Office).

Churchill, W. S. (2005), *The Hinge of Fate* (Penguin Classics).

Coram, R. (2004), *Boyd: The Fighter Pilot Who Changed the Art of War* (Little Brown).

Courtney, H., Kirkland, J. and Viguerie, P. (1997), Strategy Under Uncertainty, *Harvard Business Journal*, Nov–Dec 1997 (Harvard Business School Publishing).

Covey, S. R. (1994), *The Seven Habits of Highly Effective People* (Simon & Schuster).

Davenport, T. H. and Prusak, L. (1998), *Working Knowledge* (Harvard Business School Press).

de Bono, E. (1999), *Six Thinking Hats* (Penguin Books).

de Bono, E. (2000), *New Thinking For The New Millennium* (Penguin Books).

DeMarco, T. and Lister, T. (1999), *Peopleware: Productive Projects and Teams* (Dorset House Publishing).

— (2003), *Waltzing With Bears* (Dorset House Publishing).

DSDM Consortium (2007), *Dynamic Systems Development Method v4.2* (Tesseract Publishing).

Einhorn, H. J. and Hogarth, R. M. (1987), Decision Marking: Going Forward in Reverse, *Harvard Business Journal*, Jan–Feb 1987 (Harvard Business School Publishing).

Gershon, P. (1999), *Review of Civil Procurement in Central Government* (HM Treasury).

ten Have, S., ten Have, W., Stevens, F. and van der Elst, M. (2003), *Key Management Models* (FT Prentice Hall).

Hillson, D. and Murray-Webster, R. (2007), *Understanding and Managing Risk Attitude* (Gower Publishing).

Kylen, B. (1985), What Business Leaders Do – Before They Are Surprised, In *Advances in Strategic Management*, Volume 3, edited by Lamb, R. and Shrivastava, P. (JAI Press Inc.).

Loch, C. H., DeMeyer, A. and Pich, M. T. (2006), *Managing The Unknown* (John Wiley & Sons).

McConnell, S. (1996), *Rapid Development* (Microsoft Press).

Myddelton, D. R. (2007), *They Meant Well: Government Project Disasters* (The Institute of Economic Affairs).

Meltzer, M. (2007), *Mission to Jupiter: A History of the Galileo Project* (NASA)

Pfeffer, J. and Sutton, R. I. (2006), Evidence-Based Management, *Harvard Business Review*, January 2006 (Harvard Business School Publishing).

Peters, T. (1988), *Thriving on Chaos* (Pan Books).

Rasiel, E. M. (1998), *The McKinsey Way* (McGraw-Hill).

Reason, J. (2000), Human Error: Models and Management, *British Medical Journal*, pp. 768–770, 18th March 2000.

Richards, C. (2004), *Certain to Win, The Strategy of John Boyd, Applied to Business* (Xlibris Corporation).

Rogers, P. and Blenko, M. (2006), Who Has the D? How Clear Decision Roles Enhance Organizational Performance, *Harvard Business Journal*, Jan 2006 (Harvard Business School Publishing).

Schein, E. H. (2004), *Organizational Culture and Leadership* (The Jossey-Bass Business and Management Series), 3rd Edition (Jossey-Bass).

Schoemaker, P. J. H. (2002), *Profiting From Uncertainty* (The Free Press).

Sloane, P. (2007), *The Leader's Guide to Lateral Thinking Skills* (Kogan Page).

Walton, M. and Deming, W. E. (1992), *The Deming Management Method*, 2nd Edition (Mercury Business Books).

Weick, K. E. and Sutcliffe, K. M. (2001), *Managing The Unexpected* (Jossey-Bass).

Whyte, J. (2003), *Bad Thoughts: A Guide To Clear Thinking* (Corvo Books).

RECOMMENDED READING ON RISK MANAGEMENT

Chapman, C. and Ward, S. (1997), *Project Risk Management: Processes, Techniques and Insights* (Wiley).

Gigerenzer, G. (2003), *Reckoning With Risk* (Penguin Books).

Modarres, M. (2006), *Risk Analysis in Engineering: Techniques, Tools and Trends* (Taylor & Francis).

Remenyi, D. (1999), *Stop IT Project Failures Through Risk Management* (Butterworth Heinemann).

INDEX

80/20 principle 95, 97, 107; *see also* Pareto's Law

A
Ackoff, R. 55
adapt 38–41; *see also* confrontation mode
affordability 21–2, 37
agility 18, 89–92
ambiguity 9
anticipation strategies 17–8, 71, 101
Asimov, I. 57
association 51

B
Bernstein, P. 21
Boehm, B. 108
Bohr, N. 71
bolt from the blue 13, 23
de Bono, E. 81, 115
Boyd, J. 99–100

C
cane toad 55
Casani, J. 3–4
causal relationship; *see also* variables, relationships between
   strong 51
   weak 51
cause-and-effect chains 9
Chapman, C. 5
Churchill, W. 1–2
complexity 12, 23–4, 37, 75–6; *see also* uncertain complexity
confrontation mode 37; *see also* adapt; detour; reorient, suppress
constraints 48, 51
containment 22
creativity 18, 81, 114–6
critical path 75

D
decision making
   evidence-based 68–9
   process 65–7, 76
decision-makers 67–8
decision point 74–5, 77
decision tree 18, 76–8
DeMarco, T. 27, 114
DeMeyer, A. 5
Deming, W. E. 95
detour 38–9, 41; *see also* confrontation mode
Dickens, C 105
discovery techniques 17
DSDM 93–4
dynamic tension 102–3

E
early warning signs 16–8
Einstein, A 37
estimation methods 9, 15
evaluation criteria 49, 52
experiments 15; *see also* multiple explorations

F
fast learning loops 15, 18, 91–3
faulty assumptions 9, 14
Finagle's laws of information 21
fishbone diagram 78–9
Fleming, A. 8
forecasting model 18, 57–60, 71–6
four quadrants model 12

G
Galileo mission 3–4
gateway reviews 25

H
high reliability organizations 111, 113